The

UNWINDING
ANXIETY

Workbook

ALSO BY JUDSON BREWER, MD, PHD

The Hunger Habit
Unwinding Anxiety

The

UNWINDING
ANXIETY

Workbook

PRACTICAL EXERCISES TO BREAK THE CYCLES
OF WORRY AND FEAR AND HEAL YOUR MIND

JUDSON BREWER, MD, PhD

AVERY

an imprint of Penguin Random House

New York

AVERY

an imprint of Penguin Random House LLC
1745 Broadway, New York, NY 10019
penguinrandomhouse.com

Library of Congress Control Number: 2024943729

Trade Paperback ISBN: 9780593853016
Ebook ISBN: 9780593853023

Printed in the United States of America
1st Printing

Book design by Angie Boutin

Neither the publisher nor the author is engaged in rendering professional advice or services to the individual reader. The ideas, procedures, and suggestions contained in this book are not intended as a substitute for consulting with your physician. All matters regarding your health require medical supervision. Neither the author nor the publisher shall be liable or responsible for any loss or damage allegedly arising from any information or suggestion in this book.

The authorized representative in the EU for product safety and compliance is Penguin Random House Ireland, Morrison Chambers, 32 Nassau Street, Dublin D02 YH68, Ireland, https://eu-contact.penguin.ie.

To my wife, Mahri, who has taught me
so much over the years

Contents

Part III

FINDING THAT BIGGER, BETTER OFFER FOR YOUR BRAIN: THIRD GEAR

Introduction

I have scienced the sh*t out of anxiety.

As a behavioral neuroscientist, I have dedicated decades of research to understanding why habits form, and how we can break free of them. As a psychiatrist, I have tested and tweaked tools to help people implement meaningful change in their lives. As a person, I've had my own share of anxiety, ranging from anxiety-driven, body-exploding irritable bowel syndrome to full-blown panic attacks. And this isn't to say that I am now anxiety-free—I still have anxiety show up for me on a regular basis. But I now know how to manage my anxiety, to relate to it differently. And this has made all the difference.

A word of warning: If you are hoping this workbook or my *Unwinding Anxiety* book or for that matter any other book is going to rid you of anxiety, unfortunately you will invariably be disappointed.

This isn't how anxiety (or our brain) works. We have no "anxiety switch" that can be flipped off—oh, how we all wish there were such a thing! The good news is that once you learn how and why anxiety shows up and how you might inadvertently be stoking it, you can learn how to manage it when it appears and not feed it, so it doesn't last as long or show up as often.

I wrote this workbook to serve as a companion for *Unwinding Anxiety,* the book I published in 2021. *Unwinding Anxiety* spells out all the details, the science, and the methods for breaking free from anxiety habit loops. Think of this workbook as your trusty mule, or if you are a *Star Wars* fan, your R2-D2 sidekick: it will help you carry the load on your journey into wisdom. Reading a book—understanding concepts—doesn't get you very far. Wisdom comes only from experience. You have to do the work, put concepts into practice, in order to develop wisdom.

HOW TO USE THIS WORKBOOK: PUTTING KNOWLEDGE INTO PRACTICE

The chapters in this workbook parallel those in *Unwinding Anxiety.* If you're reading *Unwinding Anxiety,* you can read a chapter, reflect on the chapter, and then open this workbook to work through your thoughts in the spirit of that chapter. I'll summarize the main points of each chapter in *Unwinding Anxiety*, followed by suggested tips and tools that you can use to put these concepts into practice in your everyday life.

There are many prompts and questions in this book that can help you journal through your anxiety. If you like to journal, journal away—but don't get caught in the trap of thinking that just because you have an insight and write it down, this will magically change your life. You have to put those insights into practice. You have to test them out to see which nuggets are truly golden and which are fool's gold, promising you an end to suffering but not delivering, leaving you looking for more.

Ready to get started? Let's dive in!

CHAPTER 1

Anxiety Goes Viral

Since the COVID-19 pandemic, anxiety rates have skyrocketed, with a 3.9 percent increase in reported psychological distress since 2018. As we acknowledge this rise in anxious feelings, it's important to recognize that anxiety can manifest itself in incredibly diverse and often sneaky ways. It's a shape-shifter, showing up not just in the form of worry or fear, but sometimes as physical symptoms, as avoidance behaviors, and even in the subtleties of everyday decisions and reactions. In college, my anxiety manifested itself as irritable bowel syndrome. For others, it ranges from constant worry to full-blown panic attacks.

Remember, anxiety is defined as "a feeling of worry, nervousness, or unease, typically about an imminent event or something with an uncertain outcome."

It is important to be able to see and feel the difference between the feeling of worry and the mental behavior of worrying. We'll get into this more in subsequent chapters, but make sure you bookmark this in your brain now: a feeling is not a behavior.

EXERCISE 1: HOW DO YOU DISTINGUISH FEELINGS FROM BEHAVIORS?

A feeling is a subjective experience or emotional state, while a mental behavior is an action that stems from one's thoughts, feelings, or internal/external prompts. For example, anxiety is a feeling, while worrying and procrastinating are behaviors. In the grid below, write down different feelings and mental behaviors.

FEELINGS	BEHAVIORS

Anxiety is so pervasive that we often overlook its impact because it's not as visible or as straightforward as other conditions. It can be quietly woven into the fabric of our lives, showing up in our drive to succeed, in the care we take in avoiding certain foods or situations, or even in the intensity with which we pursue our hobbies and interests.

The ability to see and acknowledge the various forms of anxiety is a powerful first step in addressing them. Recognizing these patterns allows us to approach them with curiosity and kindness, to better understand their origins and the ways they influence our behavior.

Anxiety is not always the enemy; it can be a misguided attempt by our brains to protect us or to propel us forward. But when it becomes a habit loop that reinforces itself—like eating to manage anxiety, only to feel worse afterward—it's essential to step back and reevaluate its role in our lives.

How we react to anxiety also demonstrates the importance of self-compassion. We need to understand our history with anxiety and our responses to it, and learn how to navigate it without judgment. This approach isn't about eradicating anxiety; instead, it's about changing our relationship with it and, in so doing, allowing ourselves to live more fully and with greater ease.

EXERCISE 2: HOW DOES ANXIETY SHOW UP FOR YOU?

Is anxiety in your body? What does it feel like? Where do you feel it?

_____

_____

_____

_____

Is anxiety in your mind? What thoughts come up?

_____

_____

_____

_____

What else do you notice?

_____

_____

_____

_____

EXERCISE 3: HOW OFTEN DOES ANXIETY SHOW UP IN YOUR LIFE?

- ☐ It's always there
- ☐ Mornings
- ☐ Afternoons
- ☐ Night
- ☐ Just before sleep
- ☐ Daily
- ☐ Two to three times a week
- ☐ Once a week

Reflect on how often you have felt anxious:

- ☐ In the past month
- ☐ In the past six months
- ☐ In the past year
- ☐ Now, compared to five years ago

CHAPTER 2

The Birth of Anxiety

The key formula to remember for this chapter is: fear + uncertainty = anxiety.

Fear, our oldest survival tool, serves a simple purpose: it teaches us to avoid danger in the future through a mechanism known as negative reinforcement. Imagine walking into a street, almost being hit by a car, and then rushing to safety. That's fear, instant and educational. It teaches us to look both ways before crossing streets, just as our ancestors learned to avoid predators.

Our evolutionary journey as humans introduced a new layer atop our survival brain, the prefrontal cortex (PFC), which is involved in planning and creativity. The PFC predicts the future based on the past, but it needs accurate information to make these predictions. In the absence of such data, it improvises, running simulations to help us choose the best path forward (or street to cross). This is where anxiety comes in.

Anxiety is born when our PFC lacks the necessary data to predict the future accurately. Without credible information, our brains often craft fear-based narratives—after all, it's better to be safe than sorry. And unfortunately our brains remember and amplify the most shocking "news," adding to our sense of danger.

So while fear provides us with an adaptive learning mechanism meant to keep us safe, anxiety, conversely, is our overthinking brain spinning out of control due to insufficient information. The fear response is swift; anxiety, however, builds over time. Immediate survival reactions, such as jumping back onto the sidewalk to avoid an oncoming car, are instinctual and rapid. The learning that follows—like looking both ways before crossing—is quick and experiential. This is when your PFC is useful, helping you learn (and eventually plan) based on your experiences.

When it comes to anxiety, your PFC can go a bit off the rails, creating worry and concern over unlikely scenarios. It whips up a host of what-if stories that often lean toward worst-case scenarios, prompting a physiological response akin to one evoked by real danger. It can be so easy to get caught up in these stories. "What if I hadn't seen that car?" "What if . . ."

How do we deal with this? We begin by understanding how our brains work. We must recognize that uncertainty primes us for anxiety, which can spiral into panic if left unchecked. I guide my patients to see how this plays out, which helps them step back and gain a bit of comfort. But this is easier said than done; knowledge alone isn't enough.

Our brains are perpetually asking, "What if . . . ?" They can get lost in a loop when looking for answers, often resorting to speculation and fear, the prime ingredients for social contagion (especially on social media, where anything goes and fear and outrage are the soups du jour, served up daily). Remember, social contagion means that emotions are infectious. If others are anxious and tell us how worried they are, we might start to feel anxious ourselves. Don't worry: There are better ways to work with our emotions than by spreading worry across the world. To break free from anxiety, we need to develop awareness of our feelings and the outcomes they lead to. Recognizing the counterproductive nature of our reactions allows us to see their true value.

By understanding how we form anxious habits, we empower our brains to move beyond anxiety. In the end, while anxiety feeds on fear and uncertainty, just knowing this helps us begin to learn how to starve it of its power.

EXERCISE 1: FUTURE ORIENTATION

How often do you worry about the future?

- ☐ Never
- ☐ Sometimes
- ☐ Often
- ☐ Always

JOURNAL PROMPT 1: Write about a recent experience in which you felt fear. How did your body instinctively react, and what did you learn from this experience? Contrast this with a recent experience of anxiety, noting how your body felt and how your mind reacted over time. What felt similar? What felt different?

_____

_____

_____

_____

_____

JOURNAL PROMPT 2: Reflect on a decision you made recently where you had enough information to predict the outcome. How did having that information make you feel? Now think of a time when you didn't have enough information. How did that uncertainty impact your prefrontal cortex's ability to plan, and what was the result?

_____

_____

_____

_____

_____

JOURNAL PROMPT 3: Consider a time when an overload of information led you to feel anxious. Journal about the experience, focusing on how the volume and nature of the information contributed to your anxiety.

_____

_____

_____

_____

_____

JOURNAL PROMPT 4: Recall a conversation or a moment where someone else's anxiety influenced your own state of mind. Describe the contagion effect and explore how you might recognize these situations in the future so that you are less likely to catch the anxiety bug.

_____

_____

_____

_____

CHAPTER 3

Habits and Everyday Addictions

Remember this simple definition of addiction: "continuing a behavior despite adverse consequences." Many behaviors that we consider generally benign—shopping, daydreaming, checking social media, eating—if they lead to harmful results, can fit this definition.

Today addiction is everywhere, permeating modern life. It isn't limited to hard drugs or to what's conventionally understood as addictive substances. The world has changed dramatically in the past several decades, far surpassing the rate of change of the previous two centuries. Our brains are struggling to keep up, and the consequences can—but don't have to—be dire!

This isn't just about a predilection for overindulgence or a passing craze for the latest gadget. As we'll discuss in the next chapter, it's about how our ancient brains, which evolved to help us survive, are being hijacked by modern stimuli, turning survival mechanisms into harmful habits or addictions.

EXERCISE: RECOGNIZING SUBTLE ADDICTIONS

Reflect on your daily routines and identify a habit you feel compelled to repeat despite negative consequences.

How does this habit serve you in the short term, and what are the long-term impacts?

_____

_____

Are there any similarities between this habit and traditional notions of addiction?

_____

_____

Now let's consider how worrying can become a habit. Worry starts as a survival mechanism—a thought or emotion triggers a frenzy in the brain, which tries to protect us from *perceived* threats. Often worry tricks us into thinking that we are solving a problem—or at least doing something. When we're feeling anxious, doing something, even if it is worrying, often feels better than doing nothing. But this can easily become a habit loop:

- **Trigger:** An unpleasant thought or emotion (for example, feeling anxious)
- **Behavior:** Worry
- **Reward:** Temporary relief through avoidance or overplanning

Many people admit that they're addicted to worrying. But just because you fall into this habit (addiction) doesn't mean it's time to worry (more). Understanding how our minds work in this fast-paced, hyperconnected world is the first step in taking control of our habits. This knowledge is the foundation on which we can start working with our minds, rather than being at the mercy of an environment that's constantly pulling at our brain's addiction threads.

So let's take a moment to reflect. We've been focusing a lot on anxiety and worry. Sometimes it can be helpful to take a step back and look at the rest of your life, focusing on things that are less anxiety-provoking, so you can get a sense of what these habit loops and everyday addictions are like. What are the habits you continue despite adverse consequences? What daily activities might you be addicted to? Recognizing these patterns is the first step in mapping your mind and starting the journey toward managing your anxieties and breaking free from the habits that no longer serve you.

JOURNAL PROMPT 1: Think about a time when you indulged in a habit that gave you immediate pleasure or relief. Write about the "reward" your brain received, considering how it might have reinforced the behavior. Can you identify the cue and the routine that leads to this reward?

_____

_____

_____

_____

_____

_____

JOURNAL PROMPT 2: Examine how technology plays a role in your habits. Do you find yourself reaching for your phone or checking social media at specific times of the day or in certain emotional states? What might be the intermittent reinforcement you receive from these actions?

_____

_____

_____

_____

_____

_____

JOURNAL PROMPT 3: Consider a habit you have that you wouldn't classify as an addiction. What differentiates it from the addictions you see in others? Could this habit potentially have addictive qualities that you haven't acknowledged?

_____

_____

_____

_____

_____

CHAPTER 4

Anxiety as a Habit Loop

When I talk about the nature of anxiety, especially in seminars or interviews, I often notice people experiencing an aha moment when they understand that anxiety can indeed be a habit loop. To truly grasp this, we need to take a trip back in time and consider the ancient human brain.

Imagine our forebears out on the savannah. Their brains were predominantly focused on survival: obtaining food and avoiding becoming prey for predators. Venturing into new territories triggered their survival instincts, placing their senses on high alert. This was necessary, since they had no idea whether these uncharted areas were safe. Only after experiencing many safe encounters in these new areas could they relax, their brains interpreting the lack of danger as a sign of safety.

This is akin to conducting a scientific experiment. We run the same experiment multiple times, and with consistent results, we gain confidence—hence the term *confidence intervals,* which refers to the statistical measure of reliability in an experimental outcome. The brain's dislike for or intolerance of uncertainty has been a constant, from primal humans to contemporary scientists. Uncertainty signals danger, an innate "mental itch" prompting us to act. This urge can range from a minor irritation at a strange noise leading us to investigate its source to an intense drive to act in the face of imminent danger.

Remember, anxiety, by definition, is the feeling of worry, nervousness, or unease about something with an uncertain outcome. It acts as a trigger, urging us to do something—to find a solution. In this habitual loop, stress or anxiety triggers a behavior aimed at finding a solution, and sometimes hitting upon a solution offers a temporary reward by alleviating the anxiety. This mechanism is akin to gambling at a slot machine: we win just enough to keep playing.

Our brains are convinced that worry is a form of problem-solving and thus is in itself a rewarding behavior. However, the reward often falls short, since worry rarely solves the actual problem. In reality, worry is just an ineffective attempt to hit the "solution jackpot"; it actually impedes creative thinking and effective problem-solving. Why? We are afraid of the future. Put differently, we are afraid—right now, in the present moment—of something unknown occurring in the future. The problem is that we have no control over the future, so worrying doesn't keep us safe.

And how does worrying get in the way of creativity and problem-solving? Remember that the prefrontal cortex goes off-line when we're afraid. Guess what the PFC is needed for? Yup, creativity and problem-solving. Worrying is all about getting stuck in the same thought loop over and over. That is the opposite of being creative and doesn't help with problem-solving.

So worrying is a mental behavior that is often seen as problem-solving but actually leads to more anxiety—we are not solving anything and are getting more anxious in the process. This cyclical pattern is what can lead to conditions like Generalized Anxiety Disorder, where there isn't necessarily a specific cause for worry, yet the anxiety persists.

Understanding and mapping these anxiety habit loops are the first steps toward breaking the cycle because we can learn to recognize the loop's futility. Only by truly seeing the unrewarding nature of worry can we begin to untangle ourselves from its grip.

EXERCISE 1: DECONSTRUCT THE ANXIETY REWARD

1. When you engage in the behavior that follows anxiety (such as worry), ask yourself, *What is the outcome that I'm seeking?*

2. Write down if the behavior leads to the desired outcome or if it simply results in more anxiety.

_____

_____

JOURNAL PROMPT 1: Reflect on a time when you felt anxious. What triggered it? Now that you look back, was the level of anxiety proportional to the situation?

_____

_____

_____

_____

JOURNAL PROMPT 2: Consider the habit loops you've identified. Write about how these might have served you in the past. Are they still serving a purpose, or are they outdated coping mechanisms?

_____

_____

_____

_____

JOURNAL PROMPT 3: How does your anxiety speak to you? If it had a voice, what would it say, and how would you respond to it with kindness rather than frustration?

_____

_____

_____

_____

_____

JOURNAL PROMPT 4: Imagine your anxiety as a scared child. How would you comfort it? Can you apply this same compassion to yourself?

_____

_____

_____

_____

JOURNAL PROMPT 5: Write about an experience where you felt the urge to act on your anxiety but chose to respond differently. What did you do, and what was the outcome?

_____

_____

_____

_____

THE GEARS

The process of unwinding anxiety—or any pesky habit—is best explained by a three-step procedure that has more to do with bicycles than brains. Just as the gears on a mountain bike or a car help move it forward, no matter what the terrain, these three gears will help you move forward as you learn how to step out of anxiety and other habit loops for good. Here's a summary of the gears that you can bookmark and come back to any time you need to.

First Gear

First gear is all about recognizing our habit loops and seeing the different components clearly: **trigger, behavior, and reward (TBR)**. (You can also think of *reward* as *result*.) You can keep track of your habit loops in this workbook (page 30) or in a notebook or on a blank sheet of paper, beginning with the most obvious one. Don't worry about changing your habits yet. Learning how your mind works is the first step in this change—don't rush it.

Second Gear

Second gear is paying attention to the results of your actions. It is reward-based learning, or good old cause and effect (behavior = cause, result = effect). How rewarding the result is feeds back and determines whether you strengthen or weaken the habit loop. After you've identified and mapped out your habit loops in first gear, ask yourself this simple question: "What do I get from this behavior?" Answering it will require you to pay careful attention to the actual visceral embodied sensations, emotions, and thoughts that come as a result of the behavior in question.

See if you can start driving in second gear. Map out a habit loop (anxiety or otherwise) to get yourself moving; then shift into second gear by focusing on the result of the behavior. Bring your awareness into your embodied experience and consider the question *What do I get from this?* Paying attention to the way the behavior makes you feel helps you see clearly how rewarding (or unrewarding) that worry or other habit loop is right now. This updates that reward value in your brain so that you strengthen healthy habits and start to become disenchanted with those that you're trying to let go of.

Third Gear

A broad definition of third gear: Anything that helps you step out of your old habit loop.

A specific, sustainable definition of third gear: An internally based bigger, better offer (BBO) that helps you step out of your old habit loop and into the present moment.

Your brain is constantly making decisions. For example, if given a choice between cake and broccoli, which is the bigger, better offer for your brain? Once you see how unrewarding your old behavior is (second gear), it is much easier to find something better. Be careful, though: You can't step out of a loop by substituting a new habit for your current one—eating cake to distract you from your worries when you're stressed, for example. Why? See for yourself. Start by mapping out what types of BBOs you bring in as substitution strategies for your old habit. Do they feed the habit loop—that is to say, do they result in restlessness, contraction, temporary fixes, and the desire for more? Or do they help you set out on a different path?

Instead, you need to find something readily available that tackles anxiety, worry, and other habitual behaviors head on. One of my favorite BBOs is curiosity. Think about it. Which feels better, being caught up in a craving or worry, or being curious? To our brains, it's a no-brainer. Curiosity feels great.

Curiosity helps you to start building an awareness of the thoughts, emotions, and sensations that come with your habit. Instead of feeling that you must do something about them, simply getting curious from moment to moment will help you be able to work with anxiety and worry—sometimes this is all you need. You'll learn some specific curiosity practices when you get to that section of the book.

EXERCISE 2: DEFINE THE GEARS

Write out the definitions of first, second, and third gears *in your own words*.

FIRST GEAR: _____

SECOND GEAR: _____

THIRD GEAR: _____

Mapping Your Mind
First Gear

Nobody can go back and start a new beginning,
but anyone can start today and make a new ending.

—MARIA ROBINSON

CHAPTER 5

How to Map Your Mind

The first gear in the journey of understanding and working with our habits, especially those related to anxiety, is all about recognition. It's seeing the constituent parts of our habit loops: the trigger (T), the behavior (B), and the result (R), which was once a reward that reinforced the behavior. Sometimes this "reward" may not feel rewarding now, but it was sufficient to keep the loop going initially.

MIND-MAPPING EXERCISE

To gain insight, try mapping out your own habit loops. This isn't about making immediate changes; it's about learning how your mind operates. You can download a mind-mapping template from my website, or simply use a blank sheet of paper to track the TBR components of your anxiety habit loops. Start with the most apparent loops and see where this takes you.

EXERCISE 1: HABIT LOOP IDENTIFICATION

1. Use the diagrams below, or draw a large triangle on a sheet of paper and label the corners as Trigger (T), Behavior (B), and Result (R).

2. For one week, jot down every time you experience anxiety or another strong emotion. Note what prompted it (T), what you did in response (B), and what the outcome was (R).

3. After the week, review your entries and circle any patterns you notice.

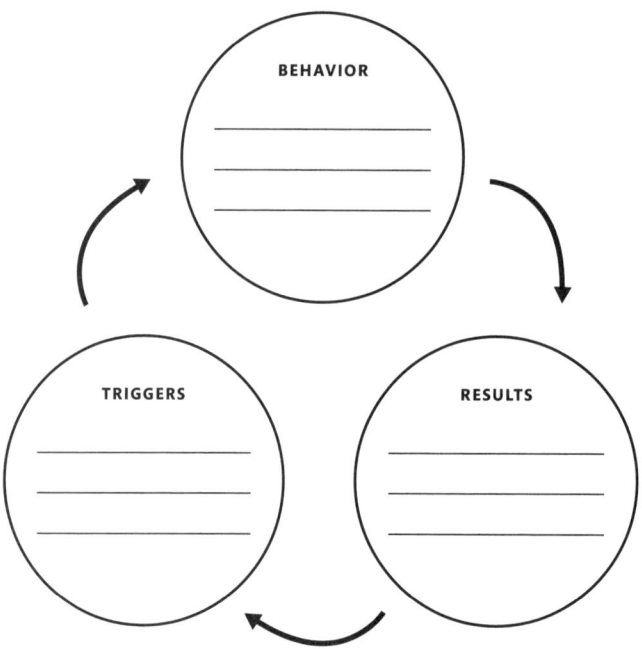

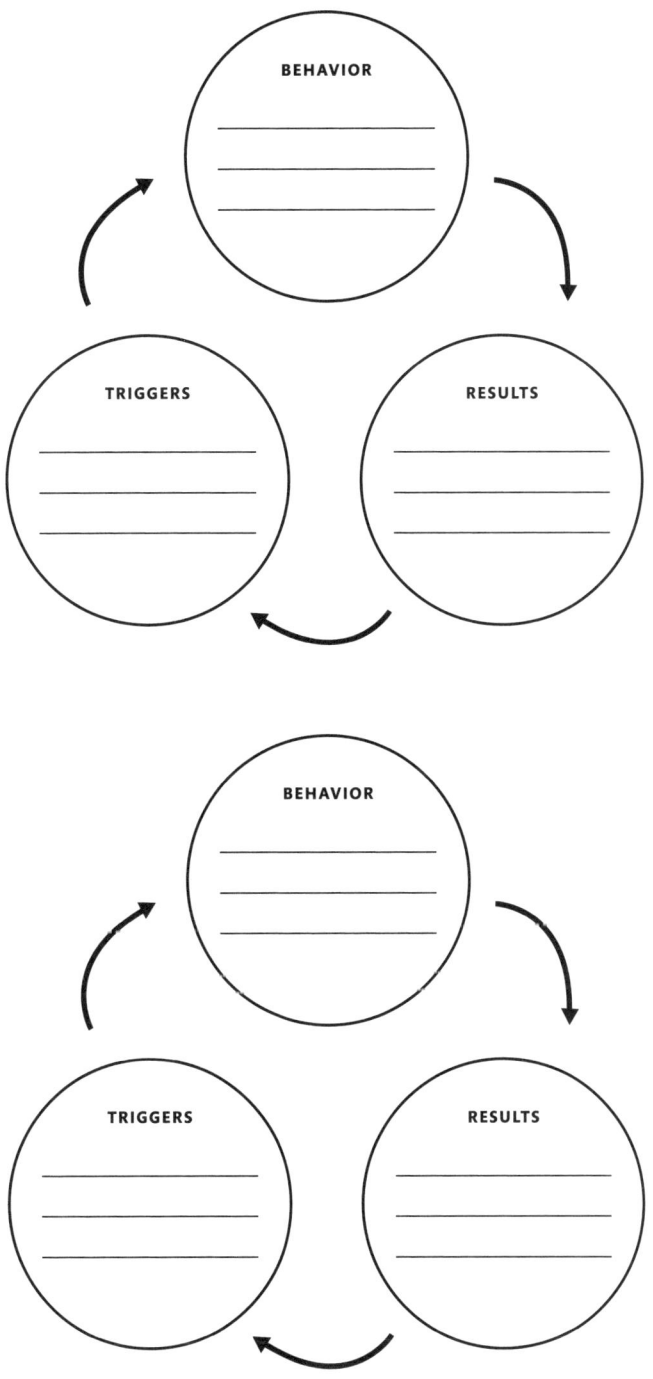

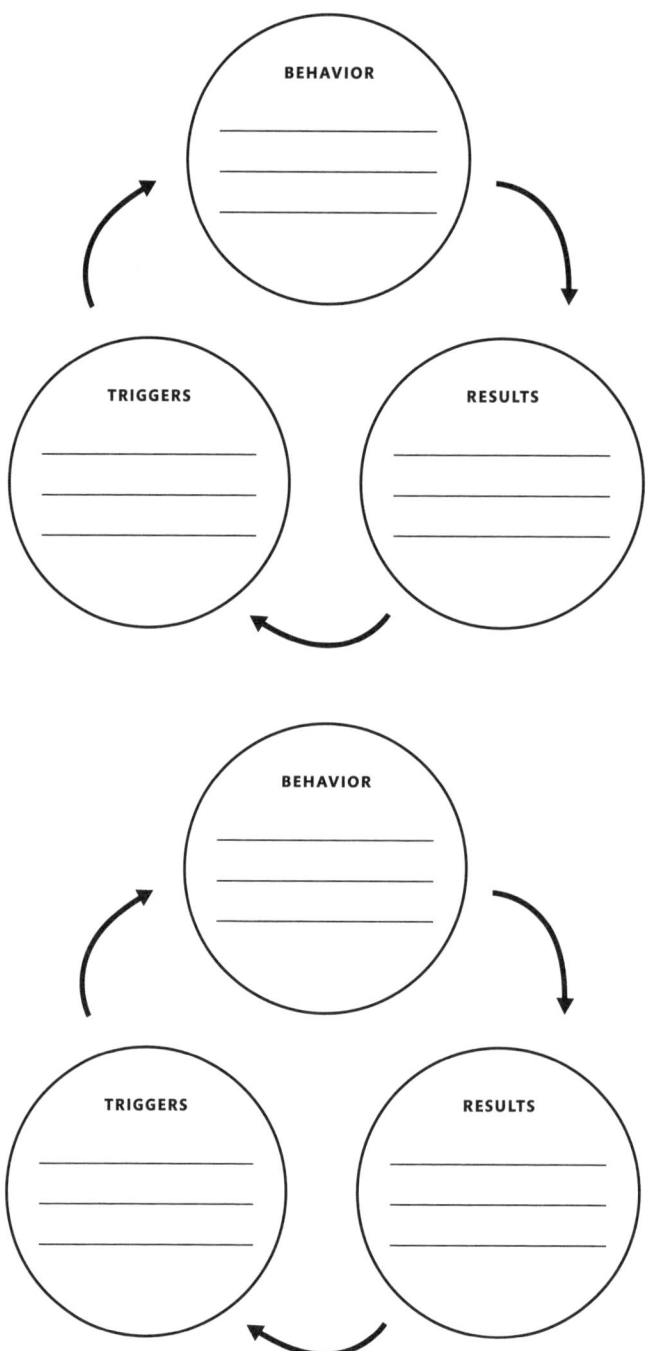

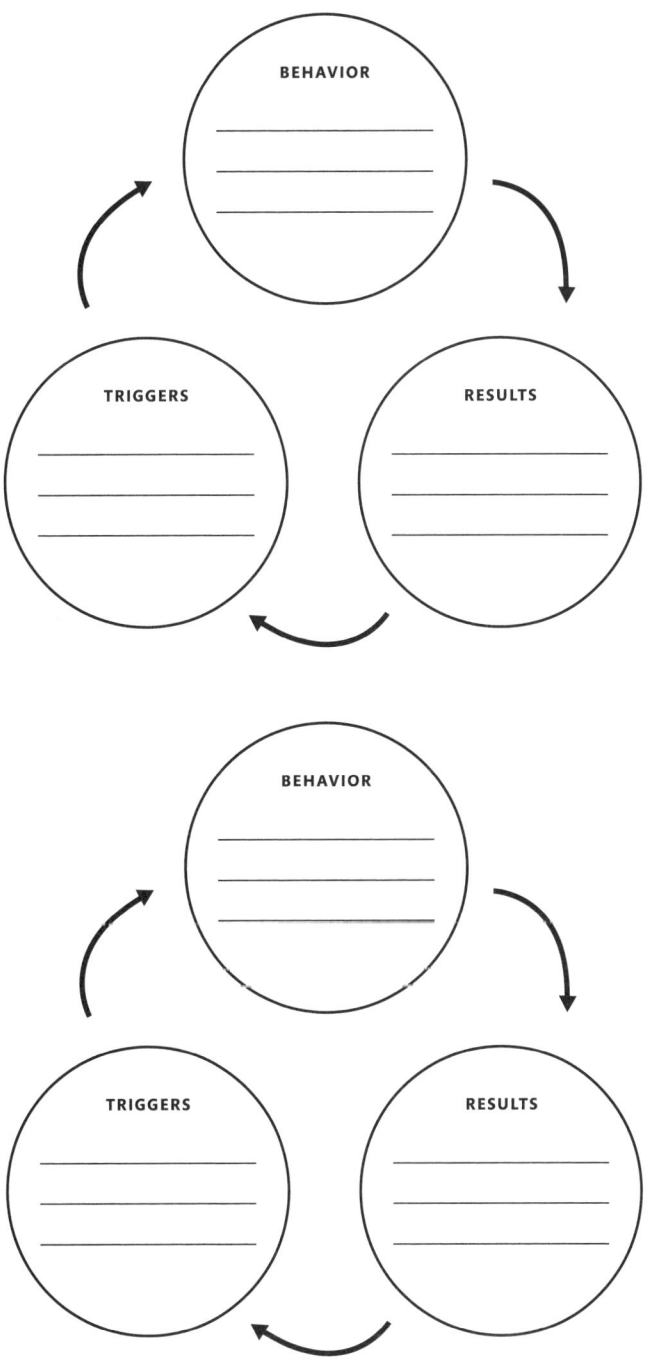

An Important Reminder

Mapping out habit loops might seem straightforward at first. But the real challenge comes when you start seeing them clearly, and you're tempted to jump right into solving them—this is a trap. It's like hearing an odd noise in your car, understanding the problem from the mechanic, and then trying to fix it yourself, which usually doesn't end well.

Remember to be on the lookout for this additional habit loop that might emerge:

☐ **Trigger:** Recognizing habit loops clearly

☐ **Behavior:** Attempting to fix them using familiar yet ineffective methods

☐ **Result:** Ineffectiveness and potentially more frustration

This is why the first section of the book is dedicated to understanding and mapping out these loops. It's essential not to rush through this process or skip ahead to the "fix" without fully grasping the mapping phase. This is the foundational work.

EXERCISE 2: AVOIDING THE FIX-IT TRAP

1. Fill in the two-column chart on the next page. In the first column, write down instances where you've tried to immediately fix a habit loop using old methods.

2. In the second column, reflect on what new knowledge or skills you would need to effectively address these loops.

3. Choose one habit loop from your list and commit to learning one new skill over the next month to address it properly.

ADDRESSING HABIT LOOPS

OLD METHODS	NEW SKILLS

RELATING TO *THE KARATE KID*

In *The Karate Kid,* Daniel LaRusso didn't just read about karate; he practiced it, translating concepts into action through experience. This is what we aim for in habit change. Understanding concepts is crucial, but it's not the same as changing a habit. It's about putting in the work, like the famous "wax on, wax off" scenes, which taught Daniel the value of embodied knowledge over mere conceptual understanding. This is what will make the concepts stick and transform them into actionable wisdom. You have to engage with the process, step by step, to truly learn and effect change.

The point is that while books, inspirational talks, and concepts in general can be exciting, even seductive, they're just a starting point. For lasting change, you must go through the mapping process experientially before you can move on to changing them. That's why a significant portion of this book is devoted to the mapping process. It's crucial not to rush this foundational step.

JOURNAL PROMPT 1: Reflect on a time when recognizing a habit loop led to a premature attempt to fix it. What was the outcome, and what did you learn from it?

_____

_____

_____

_____

_____

_____

JOURNAL PROMPT 2: Describe a situation where mapping out a habit loop has already led to positive change. How did patience play a role in this process?

_____

_____

_____

_____

JOURNAL PROMPT 3: Consider the concept of "wax on, wax off" in your life. How can you apply this idea to habit formation and the un winding of everyday habit loops beyond anxiety?

_____

_____

_____

_____

_____

_____

_____

JOURNAL PROMPT 4: Write about the feelings that arise when you think you've mastered a concept from a book or talk, but then struggle to put it into action. How can you be more patient with yourself during this process?

_____

_____

_____

_____

_____

CHAPTER 6

Why Your Previous Anti-Anxiety (and Anti-Habit) Strategies Failed

When we talk about managing anxiety and changing habits, it's critical to understand why some strategies we might have tried before may not work as well as we'd hoped. This understanding helps us navigate our anxiety habit loops, like chronic worrying, more effectively. Here's a summary of the three most common anti-habit strategies that tend to fail, and a fourth that may be more effective (hint: my lab has studied it and it works pretty well).

ANTI-HABIT STRATEGY 1: WILLPOWER

Many believe that if you have enough willpower, you can override your desires and choose healthier options. But research is increasingly questioning this idea. It seems that willpower may be more a matter of genetics for some, and for others, it's not a reliable resource at all. Efforts to exert self-control often leave people feeling more depleted, not more successful. When stressed, the prefrontal cortex, where willpower resides, often goes off-line, leaving us to fall back on our old habits, no matter our intentions. This is particularly true for anxiety, where simply telling yourself to relax often doesn't work, especially when anxiety shuts down the reasoning parts of the brain.

EXERCISE 1: WILLPOWER REALITY CHECK

1. Reflect on a recent situation where you relied on willpower to manage anxiety or change a habit.

2. Record the outcome and how you felt afterward, particularly noting any feelings of depletion or failure.

_____

_____

_____

_____

ANTI-HABIT STRATEGY 2: SUBSTITUTION

In this frequently used anti-habit strategy, the idea is to replace a harmful behavior with a less harmful one when an urge to stress-eat, worry, or otherwise do something that keeps us stuck in old habit loops. While scientifically supported and frequently used in addiction psychiatry, substitution may not address the underlying habit loop. The result is that the loop remains, just with a different behavior, which may be why people often revert to their old habits over time.

EXERCISE 2: HABIT SUBSTITUTION ANALYSIS

1. List any habits you've tried to change by substitution (e.g., eating candy instead of smoking).

2. For each, note whether the new behavior satisfied the craving or just acted as a placeholder.

3. Reflect on if the underlying habit loop is still active and brainstorm ways to address the loop itself rather than just the behavior (hint: Map it out and keep reading *Unwinding Anxiety*).

- _____

  _____

- _____

  _____

- _____
  _____

ANTI-HABIT STRATEGY 3:
PRIME YOUR ENVIRONMENT

If you're trying to make a change in your habits, you might think about mixing up your environment. Setting up your environment to support that habit change can be beneficial. But changing your environment requires getting into a new habit quickly, which can be challenging, and it doesn't prevent relapse into old habits. For example, you might sign up for a gym membership, reasoning that the gym's environment will help you get into exercise. But you still have to get to the gym first. Thus, this strategy for developing healthier habits often fails, and in actuality, gyms plan their budgets around people's failure to maintain new exercise habits beyond the first burst of New Year's resolutions.

EXERCISE 3: ENVIRONMENTAL PRIMING EVALUATION

1. Identify the ways you have primed your environment to encourage new habits or discourage old ones.

2. Assess how effective these strategies have been in the long term. Note any relapses and what may have triggered them.

3. Outline a plan to strengthen your environment priming, ensuring it supports habit change more sustainably (optional).

_____

_____

_____

_____

ANTI-HABIT STRATEGY 4: MINDFULNESS

Mindfulness, a more effective anti-habit strategy, is defined by Jon Kabat-Zinn as being present in the moment without judgment. It's more than just awareness; it's curiosity. By becoming more aware of our habits as they're happening, we can begin to question them: What set this behavior in motion? What result am I getting? Is this what I want to continue doing? This curiosity can become a reward in itself, helping to change the habit loop. (And yes, this strategy is what *Unwinding Anxiety* is based on.)

EXERCISE 4: MINDFULNESS PRACTICE

1. Set aside ten minutes each day to engage in a mindfulness practice, focusing on the present moment without judgment (more on this later).

2. Keep a log of your practice, noting any changes in your awareness of habit loops and how curiosity arises.

3. At the end of the week, review your log. Identify any insights

gained, noting how these might inform your approach to changing habits.

So when it comes to working with anxiety, remember that while conventional anti-habit strategies have their place (some more than others—don't rely on willpower!), they might not address the deeper mechanisms of habit formation. By mapping out your habit loops and applying curiosity, you stand a better chance of making lasting changes. This isn't about jumping into fixing things; it's about a deeper awareness and understanding of your habits. It's about the "wax on, wax off" of personal growth, cultivating patience and insight before jumping to solutions. Keep mapping, stay curious, and you'll be on the path to genuine change.

JOURNAL PROMPT 1: Reflect on a time when stress overpowered your willpower. How might curiosity have offered a different outcome?

_____

_____

_____

_____

_____

_____

JOURNAL PROMPT 2: Write about the feeling of craving and how substitution has or hasn't worked for you. What might be a deeper need beneath that craving?

_____

_____

_____

_____

_____

JOURNAL PROMPT 3: Consider your environment. Is there a space in your life that continually leads to undesired habits? How can you re-engineer this environment to support your goals?

_____

_____

_____

_____

_____

JOURNAL PROMPT 4: Recall a recent moment of anxiety or another strong emotion. How did bringing awareness to the experience change the intensity of it or your reaction to it?

_____

_____

_____

_____

_____

CHAPTER 7

Why Performance Anxiety Is a Trap

I can't emphasize enough how important it is to be able to tell the difference between things that occur at the same time (correlation) and things that cause other things to happen (causation). This is really hard for so many people to accept, because their brains are *convinced* that anxiety is helpful for them. After all, "Anxiety is what helped me perform well." Or is it?!

Many of us have been taught to believe that a certain amount of anxiety is beneficial—it keeps us sharp, motivated, and productive. However, to put it mildly, this idea warrants a closer examination. Our brains are association-making machines, adept at linking behaviors with outcomes, like associating cake with pleasure. But this associative brilliance has a downside—it can lead us to mistakenly link anxiety with high performance—or just getting stuff done. We think that anxiety is like coffee or whatever our preferred caffeine-delivery device is: without it we wouldn't get through our day.

This mistaken belief can be traced back to the so-called Yerkes-Dodson Law, developed by researchers Robert Yerkes and John Dodson way back in 1908, which suggests that a moderate level of arousal or stress can improve performance. However, this "law" is more folklore than fact, as the original study on Japanese dancing mice doesn't necessarily translate to human anxiety and performance. Okay, let's be honest here: (1) you can't ask mice if they're anxious, and (2) who would believe dancing mice if they could speak anyway?

While we often romanticize anxiety as a driver of success, believing that it's essential for achieving goals, modern research does not consistently support this notion. In fact, evidence suggests that stress is more often a hindrance than a help.

We may find anecdotal instances where we feel our anxiety has driven us to accomplish tasks effectively, but we must ask ourselves: Is anxiety really driving success, or is it true, true, and unrelated? I was anxious (true). X happened (true). But my anxiety didn't cause X to happen (unrelated). In other words, are we seeing/believing there is a causal relationship between anxiety and outcome where there is none? This is a vital question to consider as we move forward in changing our habits. Knowing why we've formed certain habits is less important than understanding the results that keep us stuck in said habits. As you'll learn later, knowing why a habit formed in the first place doesn't drive how we actually change it.

Sorry to put this bluntly, but it needs to be put that way: **there is** no scientific evidence suggesting that there is a type of "good anxiety." Somebody writing a popular book arguing the point doesn't count as scientific evidence.

The closest that things come to "good anxiety" is eustress. Eustress is a term that's derived from the Greek prefix *eu-* which means "good," and *stress,* obviously referring to the concept of strain or tension. Unlike *distress,* which refers to negative stress that can lead to anxiety, decrease in performance, and even health problems, eustress is associated with feelings of excitement, fulfillment, and positive challenge. It's the kind of stress you might experience when riding a roller coaster, playing a competitive game, or giving an important presentation that you're well prepared for.

So as we begin to recognize our habits, it is important to check to see if we're holding on to a story that we "need" our anxiety in order to X (X = make a deadline, perform well, etc.). When we see through the story as a story—a fairy tale with an unfortunate ending (more anxiety)—we can focus less on identifying every trigger or "needing" our anxiety and more on understanding the rewards/results that fuel these habits. This is the essence of reward-based learning, and it's where we can find the most leverage for change. By mapping out our habit loops and examining the results, we can begin to untangle the complex web of habits and find pathways to more sustainable and healthy behaviors.

EXERCISE 1: BREAKING DOWN ASSOCIATIONS

1. Identify an instance where you felt anxiety improved your performance.

2. Write down what you were anxious about, what the task was, and what happened as a result.

3. Reflect on whether the anxiety was indeed a contributing factor to your success or merely present at the time. Could it be that the success was due to your preparation, your skill, or other factors?

_____

_____

_____

_____

_____

_____

EXERCISE 2: CHALLENGING ANXIETY'S ROLE

1. Fill out the table on the following page. In the first column, identify situations where anxiety was present and you performed well.

2. In the adjacent column, identify situations where you performed well without anxiety.

3. Compare the two columns and consider the real impact of anxiety on your performance.

ANXIETY'S ROLE

PERFORMED WELL WITH ANXIETY	PERFORMED WELL WITHOUT ANXIETY

JOURNAL PROMPT 1: Reflect on how you have historically viewed anxiety in relation to success. Can you identify times when this perspective has not held true?

_____

_____

_____

_____

_____

JOURNAL PROMPT 2: Write about an occasion where you believe anxiety hindered rather than helped your performance. What might have improved the outcome?

_____

_____

_____

_____

_____

JOURNAL PROMPT 3: How has the cultural romanticization of anxiety as a badge of honor affected your life and decisions? Are there areas where you can release this belief?

_____

_____

_____

_____

_____

_____

JOURNAL PROMPT 4: Imagine your life without the association of anxiety and success. What changes in your approach to work, creativity, or personal goals?

_____

_____

_____

_____

_____

CHAPTER 8

A Brief Word on Mindfulness

Mindfulness is a concept that can be defined different ways. At the heart of it—experientially—mindfulness is about bringing a curious awareness to what is happening right now. Pragmatically, it's about observing our brain's autopilot actions and habitual patterns with clarity and insight. Often, there is confusion between mindfulness and meditation. Mindfulness is the larger practice of awareness, while meditation is a specific training to enhance mindfulness.

EXERCISE 1A

Write down all the ways you have seen mindfulness defined or portrayed in social media, magazine articles, and books.

_____

_____

_____

_____

Now circle all the phrases that ring true based on your own experience.

EXERCISE 1B

Reflect on what mindfulness means to you and how it differs from your understanding of meditation.

_____

_____

_____

_____

Mindfulness is not about achieving a special state or emptying the mind of thoughts; it's about changing our relationship with our thoughts and emotions. It's a shift from being on autopilot—where the default mode network (DMN) of the brain reigns, often leading us to ruminate on the past or worry about the future—to becoming fully aware of the present moment.

EXERCISE 2

NEVER ————————————————————————————————————— ALWAYS

Put an R on the continuum at the point that represents how much on average each day you ruminate (get stuck in the past). Put a W on the continuum at the point that represents how much on average each day you worry (about the future).

As we discussed in chapter 6, curious awareness can break the cycle of craving and rumination that are hallmarks of unhelpful habits, including anxiety. For example, understanding the prefrontal cortex's role in the default mode network allows us to see how mindfulness training can quiet these areas and potentially change unhealthy behaviors.

Let's use mindfulness to zoom in on our daily habit loops, to truly understand their structure, and to potentially rewire our brains for better outcomes. By focusing on the present, we can break free from the repetitive patterns that dominate our mental landscape.

EXERCISE 3: MINDFUL AWARENESS PRACTICE

1. Set a timer for five minutes and find a comfortable seated position.

2. Focus on your breath, noticing the sensation of air moving in and out of your body.

3. Each time you find your mind wandering, gently note whether it was a thought about the past or the future, and then return your focus to your breath.

EXERCISE 4: OBSERVING HABIT LOOPS

1. Throughout your day, take notes whenever you catch yourself in a habitual action or thought.

2. Later, review these notes to identify the trigger, the behavior, and the result of these habit loops.

3. Reflect on how awareness of these patterns might affect your behavior.

JOURNAL PROMPT 1: Describe how the concept of mindfulness challenges or supports your existing coping mechanisms for stress or anxiety.

_____

_____

_____

_____

_____

_____

JOURNAL PROMPT 2: Consider the role of the PFC and the DMN in craving and addiction. How might mindfulness alter these brain activities in your experience?

_____

_____

_____

_____

_____

Remember, mindfulness is a journey of exploration and discovery, where each moment of awareness can be a step toward greater clarity and peace.

CHAPTER 9

What Is Your Mindfulness Personality Type?

From the simplest of organisms to more complex creatures like us, many of life's activities boil down to fundamental survival strategies: our fight, flight, or freeze responses.

Interestingly, a couple of years ago, a fifth-century meditation manual was discovered discussing fight, flight, and freeze. The manual outlined how many habitual behaviors and mental personality traits could be categorized into fight/flight/freeze responses. And the writer actually used this categorization to match meditative practices to people's response tendencies.

Modern research continues to affirm this categorization of responses. These buckets lined up so well with current science that we made a modern-day measure and used psychometric research methods to validate our behavioral tendencies questionnaire (BTQ) that anyone can take (it's only thirteen questions). In today's world, people tend to fall into these same behavioral buckets. In the approach/fight bucket, you may be more motivated by rewards. If you're in the avoid/flight bucket, you're likely motivated by behaviors that are negatively reinforcing. And if you're in the freeze bucket, you fall in between these two. This aligns with reward-based learning, forming a framework we can use to understand our actions—and reactions.

Recognizing these tendencies is not about labeling ourselves but understanding our patterns so that we can live and work more harmoniously. Knowing whether we tend toward approach, avoid, or go with the flow can help us maximize our strengths and minimize setbacks.

Let's dive into exercises and prompts that help explore these tendencies and how they influence our habits and personality.

EXERCISE 1: DISCOVER YOUR TENDENCY

1. Complete the Behavioral Tendencies Quiz (page 155).

2. Reflect on your results. Do they align with your perception of your behaviors?

3. Write down specific instances where your primary behavioral tendency has shown up in your actions.

_____

_____

_____

_____

_____

EXERCISE 2: APPROACH, AVOID, OR FREEZE?

1. Think of a challenging situation you recently faced. Which tendency did you default to?

APPROACH

AVOID

GO WITH THE FLOW

2. Write down the outcomes of reacting with this tendency. Were they helpful, unhelpful, or mixed?

_____

_____

_____

EXERCISE 3: LEVERAGE YOUR TENDENCY

1. As you go through your day, identify the strengths of your primary tendency and list ways you can use them to your advantage in personal and professional settings.

2. Note down any potential pitfalls of your tendency and how you can mitigate them.

JOURNAL PROMPT 1: Reflect on how your primary behavioral tendency has shaped your relationships with others.

JOURNAL PROMPT 2: How does understanding your behavioral tendency impact your view on habit formation and change?

JOURNAL PROMPT 3: Reflect on how your tendency might influence your response to stress and anxiety.

JOURNAL PROMPT 4: Consider situations where stepping out of your habitual tendency has or could benefit you.

Remember, understanding our basic behavioral tendencies is a vital step toward self-awareness and habit change. These tendencies, when recognized and managed wisely, can be powerful tools in shaping more fulfilling lives and breaking free from unhelpful patterns.

PART 1 SUMMARY

Now that you've spent some time learning, practicing, mapping out, and reflecting on habit loops, let's get first gear into your brain on your own terms.

So now, based on what you've read and explored in your own experience, write out your own personal definition of first gear.

FIRST GEAR: _____

_____

_____

Updating Our Brain's Reward Value
Second Gear

1. You must let the pain visit.
2. You must allow it to teach you.
3. You must not allow it overstay.

—IJEOMA UMEBINYUO

CHAPTER 10

The OFC: How Your Brain Makes Decisions

The orbitofrontal cortex (OFC) is one of the most important factors in unwinding anxiety. The OFC is a crossroads in the brain where emotional, sensory, and previous behavior information gets integrated. It's where your brain sets its priorities and makes decisions for the day. Behaviors become habits when your brain deems them highly rewarding, usually when they are associated with survival. For example, in the case of something like cake, our bodies associate it with a high caloric content, and therefore see it as a reward. But the reward value of a habit isn't fixed solely on the reward itself. It can also include the context and feelings associated with it, like the joy of parties where cake was served. All this information is integrated in the OFC, where your brain sets the composite reward value of behaviors so we can quickly recall it in the future.

To break a bad habit loop, it's crucial that our brain learns to update the reward value of that habit. And the key to updating reward value is awareness. When we pay close attention to our behaviors and their results, we provide our brain with new, present-moment information that can reset old reward values and push better behaviors higher in the reward hierarchy.

By becoming more aware and thus disenchanted with the actual results of unhelpful behaviors, we can tap into the power of **the second gear of change: the act of paying attention to the direct results of actions.** Taking time to pay attention allows our brains to reassess the true reward value of our habits.

EXERCISE 1: NOTICING THE REWARD VALUES

1. Identify a habit you want to change and the perceived reward for this behavior.

2. Engage in this habit while paying close attention to the actual experience, especially the less pleasant aspects.

3. Write down the observed difference between the perceived reward and actual reward of the behavior.

_____

_____

_____

EXERCISE 2: THE MINDFUL WORRYING EXERCISE

1. Choose a topic that you usually worry about.

2. Bring in the thoughts (or whatever) that trigger the worrying, and let your brain start worrying.

3. After a little while, drop into your body to see what the results of your worrying are.

4. Check in with your mind to see if the worrying solved a problem, kept someone safe, or did whatever your brain thought it was going to help with.

5. Reflect on whether its reward value changes when you pay close attention to the worrying experience.

EXERCISE 3: RESETTING REWARDS

1. Pick a behavior you'd like to stop, such as mindless scrolling on your phone.

2. Each time you find yourself engaging in the behavior, pause and ask yourself, *What do I get from this?*

3. Record the immediate and subsequent feelings, and notice if your inclination toward the behavior changes over time.

JOURNAL PROMPT 1: Reflect on an occasion when you became aware of a habit's actual reward and how that awareness influenced your behavior.

_____

_____

_____

_____

_____

JOURNAL PROMPT 2: How has the recognition of true reward values shifted your perspective on certain foods, activities, or behaviors?

_____

_____

_____

_____

_____

JOURNAL PROMPT 3: Consider the concept of disenchantment. How can recognizing the true impact of your habits empower you to make healthier choices (for example, let go of worrying)?

_____

_____

_____

_____

_____

By integrating awareness into our daily habits, we can reassess their true reward value and potentially reshape our behaviors away from unhelpful habits into more fulfilling and healthier patterns.

CHAPTER 11

Stop Thinking

If only it were as easy as telling ourselves to stop worrying, but unfortunately, that's not how our brains work. And this is where the real work begins . . .

Moving into the second gear of habit change is not easy. It involves closely examining the outcomes of our habits, which can often be uncomfortable or even painful. However, this is a critical step that leads to disenchantment with the process itself. Our brains are wired to minimize pain for survival, so facing the discomfort that comes with changing habits can feel counterintuitive and can lead to a desire for immediate relief. This is where we may find ourselves sliding back into old patterns instead of progressing.

This pushback from our brains against the discomfort of change is where patience becomes pivotal. Obviously, habits built over a lifetime won't dissipate overnight. Just as a scientist doesn't draw conclusions from a single data point, we, too, must gather "data" repeatedly over time to form new habits. The more frequently we practice awareness and feel disenchanted with an unhelpful habit, the stronger the new neural pathway becomes, signaling "this isn't rewarding" until it becomes our new automatic response.

Remember, change can be scary. Our brains are wired to be on the lookout for danger whenever something is different.

EXERCISE 1: MAPPING OUT THE PAIN POINTS

1. Identify a habit you want to change.

2. Each time you engage in this habit, note the immediate negative outcomes to start forming a "data set" of pain points.

To incorporate this process into your life effectively, think of your daily life as your mental gym, taking moments throughout your day to practice awareness—this is the "short moments, many times" approach. Like physical exercise, mental training benefits from repetition and consistency.

EXERCISE 2: THE PATIENCE LOG

1. Keep a daily log of instances where you feel the urge to see immediate results in the process of habit change.

2. Reflect on the reasons for your impatience.

3. Reflect on whether impatience helps the process of change.

4. Notice what impatience feels like in your body as you go throughout your day.

EXERCISE 3: DISENCHANTMENT DIARY

1. Write about your experiences as you observe your habits and start to feel disenchanted with them.

2. Note any resistance or discomfort that arises and pay attention to how it changes over time.

_____

_____

_____

_____

_____

EXERCISE 4: THE "SHORT MOMENTS, MANY TIMES" TRACKER

1. Throughout the day, take short moments to be aware of your habits.

2. Track these instances to ensure you're practicing many times a day.

JOURNAL PROMPT 1: Write about the discomfort you've faced when trying to change a habit and how you navigated that experience.

_____

_____

_____

_____

_____

_____

JOURNAL PROMPT 2: Describe an instance when being patient led to better outcomes in the long term.

_____

_____

_____

_____

_____

JOURNAL PROMPT 3: When have you felt disenchanted with the disenchantment process itself? How did you work through that feeling?

_____

_____

_____

_____

JOURNAL PROMPT 4: Describe a "pain point" from an unhelpful habit. How has acknowledging it repeatedly helped disenchant that habit for you?

_____

_____

_____

_____

JOURNAL PROMPT 5: Consider a habit you're trying to change. How does mapping out the immediate results each time affect your willingness to engage in that habit again?

_____

_____

_____

_____

_____

Through these exercises and journal prompts, we begin to develop the mental fortitude required to be with and lean into the discomfort of change, laying the groundwork for new, healthier habits. It's about consistent practice and patience, allowing the experience of disenchantment to guide us toward growth.

CHAPTER 12

Retrospective Second Gear: Learning from the Past

Reflecting on our behaviors and their results—whether in the moment or afterward—is a vital part of learning and growth. This process, which I refer to as "retrospective second gear," allows us to ask ourselves, *What did I get from this?* even after an event has occurred. It's a way to glean insights from past actions and their outcomes to inform future decisions. This practice is not about dwelling on what we should have done; it's about observing and understanding the actual outcomes—how rewarding or unrewarding they truly were—and learning from them.

When we look back on our actions, especially those that lead to undesirable outcomes like overindulgence or stress, we often engage in a mental narrative filled with "shoulds," which can cloud our ability to see things clearly. Instead, if we strip away this narrative and focus on the raw experience—the "juiciness" of the sensations, emotions, and thoughts—we can get to the core of the experience. This embodied, felt experience gives us the data we need to reassess the reward value of our actions. And it's within this reevaluation where true change can begin.

For example, binge-eating after an argument can leave one feeling awful the next day—physically, emotionally, and mentally. When we retrospectively explore the trigger (the argument), the behavior (bingeing), and the result (feeling awful), we can start to see these actions not as failures, but as learning opportunities.

EXERCISE 1: MAPPING THE MOMENTS

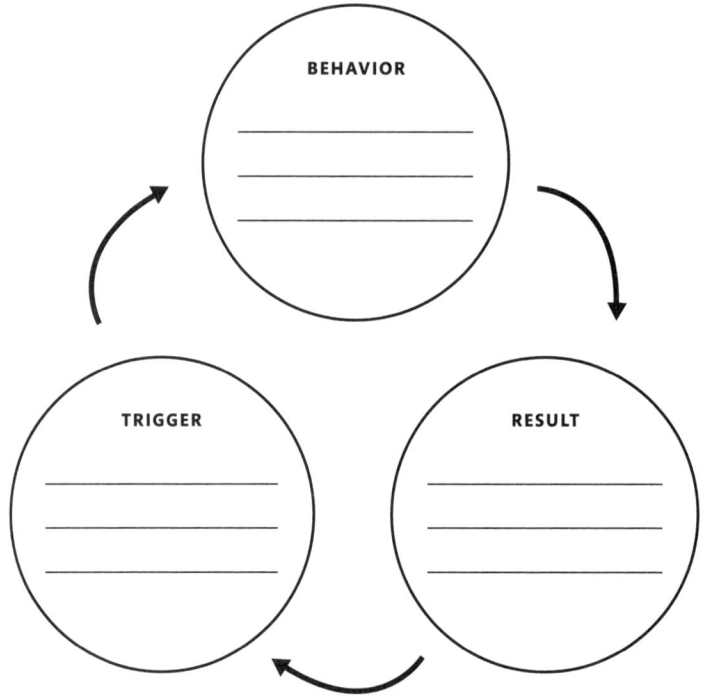

1. Map out a habit loop you've recently engaged in, focusing on the trigger, behavior, and result.

2. Reflect on the immediate sensations and emotions that followed the behavior.

Mindset is crucial in how effectively we can use retrospective second gear. A **fixed mindset**, which views abilities and intelligence as static, can lead us to interpret failures negatively, reinforcing our negative behaviors. A **growth mindset**, on the other hand, sees failure as a chance for development and learning. It's in this space that we can embrace our experiences, even the challenging ones, as teachers.

I encourage my patients to see their struggles as opportunities for growth. For instance, a patient who had been struggling with alcohol addiction saw incremental progress as failure, because she couldn't achieve complete sobriety right away. However, upon reevaluating her journey with a growth mindset, she could see that every "slipup" was a chance to learn and therefore a step forward rather than backward.

As we navigate through our habits and behaviors, remember that every moment, every action, has the potential to teach us something valuable. By approaching life with curiosity and an openness to learn, we foster a growth mindset that turns each experience, regardless of its immediate outcome, into a stepping-stone toward greater understanding and mastery over our habits.

EXERCISE 2: THE REWIND TECHNIQUE

1. Think of a habit you'd like to change.

2. Recall the last time you engaged in this habit and the subsequent results.

3. Write down your observations without judgment, focusing solely on the physical and emotional aftermath.

_____

_____

_____

_____

EXERCISE 3: GROWTH MINDSET REFRAMING

1. Identify a situation where you defaulted to a fixed mindset.

2. Write down how this mindset impacted your behavior and results.

_____

_____

_____

_____

3. Now reframe the situation through the lens of a growth mindset and note how your perception changes.

_____

_____

_____

_____

EXERCISE 4: THE HINDSIGHT PERSPECTIVE

1. Reflect on an old habit. How did it serve you in the past as opposed to how it serves you now?

2. Consider how your understanding of its reward has changed over time.

JOURNAL PROMPT 1: What recent experience, initially viewed as a setback, can you reframe as a learning opportunity?

_____

_____

_____

_____

JOURNAL PROMPT 2: How does the sensation of opening up to new perspectives feel in your body compared to when you shut down or resist change?

_____

_____

_____

_____

_____

JOURNAL PROMPT 3: In what areas of your life can you apply the lessons learned from retrospective second gear to foster growth?

_____

_____

_____

_____

Through these exercises and prompts, we can begin to harness the power of retrospective second gear, allowing our experiences to guide us toward deeper wisdom and effective change.

CHAPTER 13

Fixing the Chocolate Fix

More of a good thing is not always good. Chocolate tastes good until we've eaten so much that it tastes disgusting. Dr. Dana Small's chocolate experiment illustrates how we can shift from desire to disgust. The implication of this for changing habits is weighty, especially in the context of habits such as overeating or worrying. It suggests that by paying attention to when pleasure turns to discomfort, we can stop the cycle of indulgence. As we've pointed out in previous chapters, it's not about willpower; it's about being aware (curious!).

EXERCISE 1: AWARENESS SCALE

1. Next time you indulge in a favorite food, use a scale of 0–10 to

rate your enjoyment from beginning to end (0 = not enjoyable at all, 10 = very enjoyable).

2. Pay special attention to the point where your enjoyment starts to diminish (that is to say, below 5).

How we form habits also applies to how our attitudes shape our actions and character. A negative mindset can transform even a neutral task like taking out the trash into an unpleasant experience, while a neutral or positive attitude makes it a nonissue. The way we approach our struggles—for example, with anxiety, frustration, or another difficult emotion—can either perpetuate or break our habit loops. If we adopt a playful curiosity, we may find that these emotions and thoughts have less power over us, and we can even learn from them.

When we are trying to change a habit, the attitude we bring to the table is everything. If we confront our habits with fear or frustration, we may reinforce the negative habit loop. However, by approaching them with kindness and curiosity, we can learn to see these thoughts and emotions as transient, not as fundamental to who we are. Curiosity helps us observe thoughts and emotions (this is an anxious thought) instead of being identified with them (I'm an anxious person).

EXERCISE 2: ATTITUDE ADJUSTMENT

1. Choose a mundane or unpleasant task.

2. Perform the task once with a negative attitude and once with a positive or neutral attitude.

3. Reflect on the difference in your experience.

EXERCISE 3: THE CURIOSITY SHIFT

1. When facing a habitual reaction, like frustration, pause to explore the sensation with curiosity.

2. Write down what you observe and how the reaction changes when approached playfully.

_____

_____

_____

_____

EXERCISE 4: TEACHER THOUGHTS

1. Identify a recurring negative thought.

2. Ask yourself, *What can this thought teach me?*

3. Write about the insights you gain. How can you use them for growth?

_____

_____

_____

_____

JOURNAL PROMPT 1: How can you use Dr. Small's chocolate experiment as a metaphor for your own habits of overindulgence?

_____

_____

_____

JOURNAL PROMPT 2: What habitual negative attitudes do you hold toward everyday tasks, and what helps you change them?

_____

_____

_____

_____

JOURNAL PROMPT 3: In what ways can you use your emotions and thoughts as teachers rather than obstacles?

_____

_____

_____

_____

JOURNAL PROMPT 4: How do curiosity and kindness change your experience of working through a difficult habit loop?

_____

_____

_____

By engaging with these exercises and prompts, you can explore the dynamic relationship between awareness, attitude, and habit change, harnessing the brain's learning mechanisms to your advantage.

CHAPTER 14

How Long Does It Take to Change a Habit?

Y ou may have heard the myth that a new habit can be developed, or an old habit changed, in 21 days. I'm sorry to have to burst your bubble, but this isn't the truth. Dr. Maxwell Maltz's observations, while widely disseminated—largely by social media—lack empirical backing from peer-reviewed studies. True habit formation is a complex interplay of numerous factors, from genetics to context.

Few people like messiness when it comes to studies and data, but in fact one study showed that it can take anywhere from 18 to a staggering 254 days to form a habit, indicating a vast and variable landscape of being human. There's no one-size-fits-all timeline for developing or altering habits.

What truly influences habit change is the reward value associated with the behavior. This is where the Rescorla-Wagner model comes into play, presenting a mathematical explanation of how reward values update and thus influence our behavior. As a reminder, the Rescorla-Wagner model is a theory in psychology that explains how animals and humans learn to predict events by adjusting their expectations based on the difference between what they expect to happen and what actually occurs. When you indulge in an activity like eating cake, your brain establishes a reward value for that experience. If repeated actions don't align with the expected reward—such as the diminishing pleasure of eating too much cake—your brain will register a prediction error and adjust the reward value accordingly. This recalibration is at the heart of the second gear in behavior change.

My lab's research has taken these theories into the real world, using apps to study the changing reward values associated with overeating and smoking. Participants would record their cravings, then mindfully engage in the craved behavior, subsequently noting their level of contentment. This method of mindful attention provided the brain with the precise, present-moment information needed to reassess the true reward value of the behavior. Remarkably, we found that after about ten to fifteen mindful engagements, the reward value dropped significantly, aiding in the disruption of habit loops.

By practicing mindfulness—both in the present moment and retrospectively—we can reshape our brains' reward systems, moving away from "meh" toward a decisive "no thanks." For those who find themselves struggling with this process, remember, it's not about immediate behavior change. Hang tight—we'll get into that more in Part 3.

If you're experiencing self-judgment habit loops in response to feeling like you've failed at breaking anxiety or worry habit loops, it's essential to map them out and question what you truly gain from self-flagellation. By observing the pain caused by beating yourself up, you begin to break free from *this* cycle. It's about transitioning from a fixed mindset to a growth mindset, learning from each experience as you would from a teacher rather than from a tormentor.

EXERCISE 1: MINDFUL ENGAGEMENT

Engage in a habit you wish to change, but do so mindfully, noting the point of diminishing returns.

EXERCISE 2: PREDICTION ERROR LOG

When indulging in a habit, record your expected versus actual enjoyment to notice prediction errors (positive or negative).

JOURNAL PROMPT 1: How does your understanding of the Rescorla-Wagner model influence your approach to habit change?

_____

_____

_____

_____

JOURNAL PROMPT 2: Can you identify times when you've experienced prediction errors in your behavior? How did that change your actions?

_____

_____

_____

_____

_____

_____

JOURNAL PROMPT 3: In what ways do you beat yourself up over past behaviors, and what alternative healthier response can you adopt?

_____

_____

_____

_____

_____

_____

JOURNAL PROMPT 4: How can adopting a growth mindset over a fixed mindset change your ability to overcome unwanted habits?

_____

_____

_____

_____

_____

By engaging with these exercises and reflections, you're equipping yourself with the tools to navigate the complex journey of habit formation, steering clear of arbitrary timelines and focusing on the nuanced, rewarding process of change.

PART 2 SUMMARY

Second gear, in the context of my work, refers to the mindful awareness of our actions and their immediate results. It's a crucial step toward understanding and changing our habits. By consistently applying this awareness, you give your brain new information. It learns that the behavior may not be as rewarding as it originally thought, which can decrease the craving or urge to engage in the habit. This updating of the reward value is how you start to untangle old habits and form new, healthier ones. The essence of second gear is using awareness to learn from your experiences and adjusting your actions accordingly, based on a clear understanding of what's truly rewarding to you now, not just what was rewarding in the past.

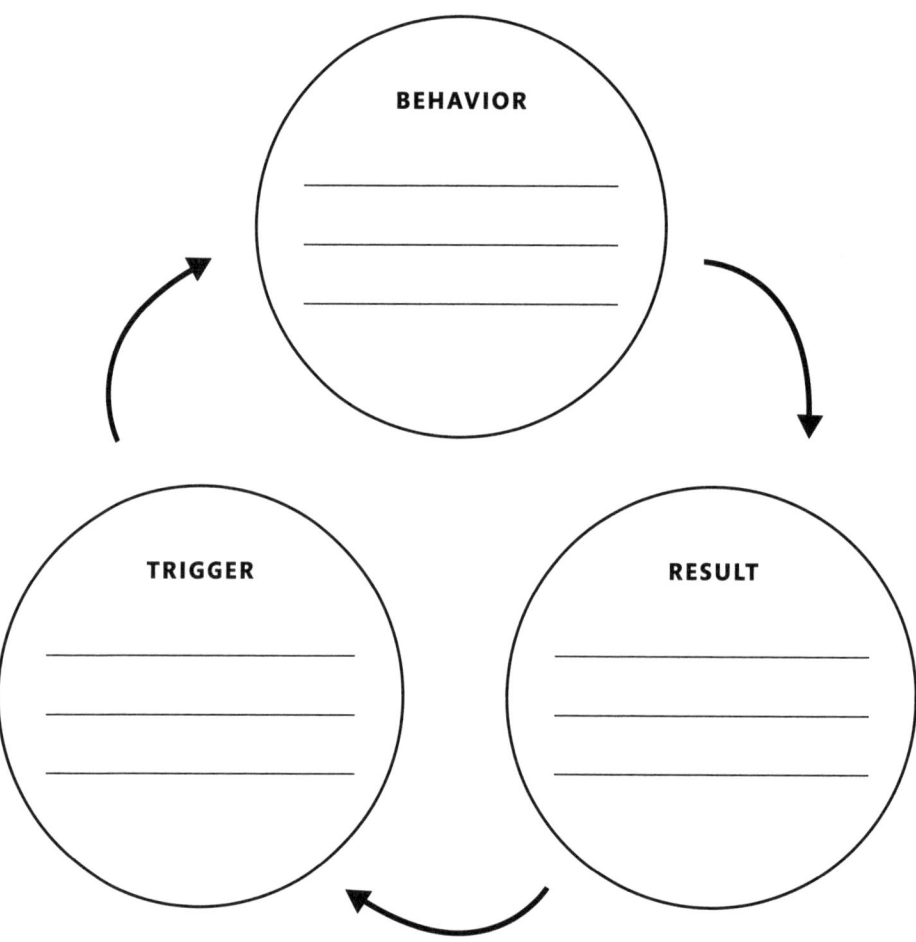

And as a reminder, change can be scary (especially when we have to bring awareness to something unpleasant).

EXERCISE: DANGEROUS OR DIFFERENT?

1. Identify a habit you want to change.

2. Map it out (first gear).

3. Check the results by asking yourself, *What am I getting from this?* (second gear).

4. Check for resistance to changing the habit, and ask, *Is this dangerous or just different?* That is to say, *Am I actually in danger, or is this just different from what I'm used to?*

5. Check for danger, and if there isn't any, see if you can use curiosity to help you lean into the discomfort of change.

Part III

Finding That Bigger, Better Offer for Your Brain

Third Gear

Curiosity will conquer fear even more than bravery will.

—JAMES STEPHENS

CHAPTER 15

The Bigger, Better Offer

In this journey, we've been using first and second gear: mapping our habit loops and becoming acutely aware of the results of our behaviors. Now we're ready to shift into third gear, where we find bigger and better offers (BBOs) that aren't just substitutions, but entirely new, internally driven behaviors that can replace our harmful urges.

Here's the definition of third gear for easy reference: a BBO that helps you step out of your old habit loop.

The best BBOs are those that become new habits and are intrinsically rewarding—the reward comes from within ourselves (hint: curiosity and kindness).

Third gear is about moving beyond substituting one habit for another. It's about finding an internally based BBO, like mindful curiosity, that doesn't just replace the old behavior but transforms our relationship to it. Instead of fighting the impulse, we harness its energy through awareness, which eventually leads to a more harmonious relationship where impulse and restraint are no longer at odds.

EXERCISE

1. Identify a habit loop you'd like to change. Write down the trigger, the behavior, and the result. Reflect on how this loop has affected you and how you feel about changing it (first gear).

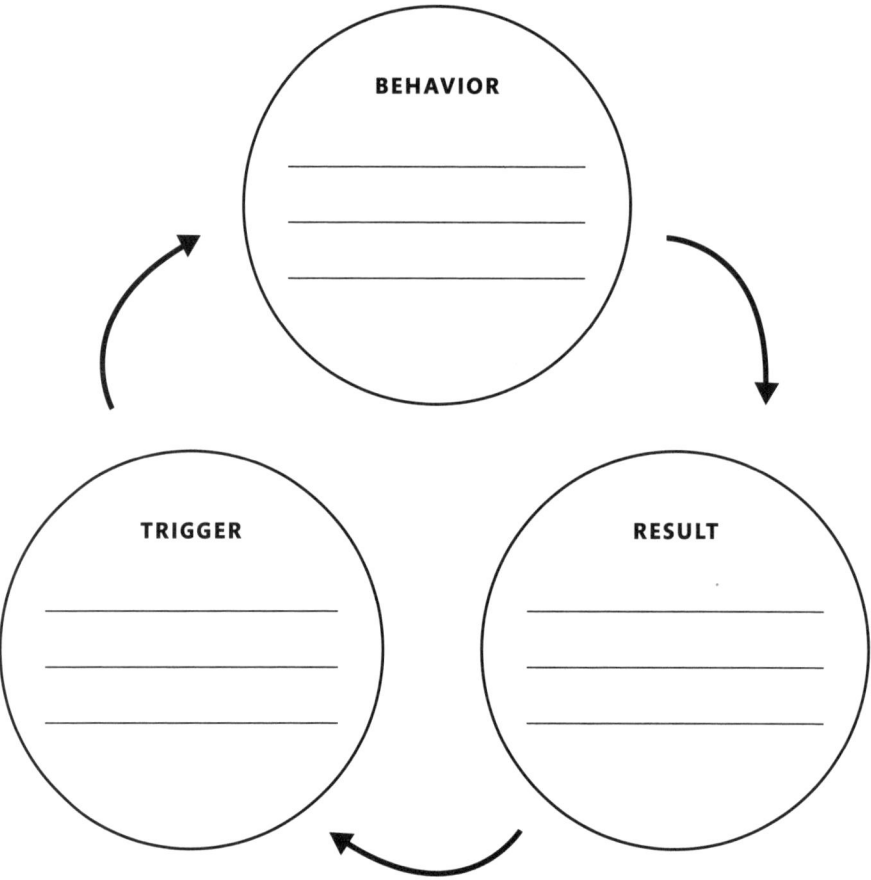

2. Think about a behavior that no longer serves you. Recall when you last engaged in this behavior and how it made you feel afterward. Write about that experience and reflect on its reward value now (second gear).

3. **Finding Your BBO:** Brainstorm a list of things you find genuinely rewarding that could serve as a healthy alternative to your habit loop. These should be internally driven and make you feel good without causing further craving or habituation.

Now, as we move forward, we'll learn how to integrate these practices more deeply into our lives, allowing mindfulness to be not just a practice but a way of living that's inherently rewarding and self-sustaining.

JOURNAL PROMPT 1: Reflect on a habit you consider rewarding. Has the reward changed over time? Does it still bring the same satisfaction?

_____

_____

_____

_____

_____

JOURNAL PROMPT 2: Journal about a disenchanting experience with a habit. What did it teach you about the true nature of that behavior's reward?

_____

_____

_____

_____

JOURNAL PROMPT 3: Think of a situation where you successfully implemented a BBO. How did it compare to the old habit in terms of satisfaction and long-term effects?

_____

_____

_____

_____

CHAPTER 16

The Science of Curiosity

I have no special talents. I am only passionately curious.

—ALBERT EINSTEIN

Curiosity propels us forward, underpinning our quest for knowledge and the joy of discovery. However, not all curiosity is equal or historically regarded as virtuous.

It is critical to know and explore the two distinct types of curiosity: I-curiosity (interest) and D-curiosity (deprivation). I-curiosity is the pleasurable pursuit of knowledge, an open-ended exploration driven by interest. On the other hand, D-curiosity is the uncomfortable need to fill information gaps, a craving for specific data that can cause restlessness until satisfied (hence its name).

For example, D-curiosity manifests when we can't recall the name attached to a familiar face or we're anticipating a text message; the tension subsides only when the information becomes available to you (you remember the name, or the text message finally comes in). Interest curiosity is different; it's the delight in learning something new and unexpected, like marveling over the fact that some animals continue to grow throughout their lives.

Curiosity intertwines with reward-based learning, which relies on positive and negative reinforcements. Just as we crave food and water, our brains also hunger for information, vital for planning and predicting. This has been demonstrated in studies where heightened curiosity enhances memory and learning, revealing dopamine's role in fostering knowledge acquisition.

Yet these two forms of curiosity yield different experiences and rewards. Deprivation curiosity provides relief from an unpleasant state, while interest curiosity is an inherently rewarding journey of discovery. I-curiosity, unlike D-curiosity, doesn't habituate or diminish over time, offering endless potential for personal growth.

EXERCISE 1: CURIOSITY IDENTIFICATION

Reflect on your recent experiences with curiosity. Categorize those experiences as I-curiosity or D-curiosity. Note the different sensations and outcomes associated with each.

In habit change, we often approach problems with D-curiosity alone, seeking solutions and perhaps feeling tense as we work to find the right solution. But leveraging both I-curiosity and D-curiosity in habit change allows us to break old habits and forge new ones. By understanding how our brains work and engaging with our experiences curiously, we can stay perched on the sweet spot of the curiosity knowledge curve, avoiding frustration and lack of interest.

CURIOSITY IS A SUPERPOWER

To practice curiosity, we can use a curiosity exercise. This involves recalling a recent habit loop, focusing on the urge before acting, and observing it with a curious mind. By labeling the sensation and watching it with a sense of wonder, we can transform our experience. Curiosity then shifts from an abstract concept to a tangible, powerful force that we can use to work with anxiety and unwind unhelpful habit loops.

EXERCISE 2: CURIOSITY TRACKING

Throughout the day, observe moments of curiosity, noting when they occur and the quality of interest or deprivation they hold.

EXERCISE 3: CURIOSITY SWITCH

When feeling an urge related to a habit loop, deliberately switch from D-curiosity (needing to know or do something) to I-curiosity (exploring the sensations and experience without judgment).

JOURNAL PROMPT 1: Recall a moment from childhood where curiosity led you to a fascinating discovery. How does that compare to your adult experiences with curiosity?

_____

_____

_____

_____

JOURNAL PROMPT 2: When was the last time you experienced a strong sense of D-curiosity, and how did you resolve it (that is to say, how did you scratch the itch of not knowing)?

_____

_____

_____

_____

JOURNAL PROMPT 3: Journal about a stressful situation in which approaching it with I-curiosity rather than a need to immediately resolve it changed the experience.

_____

_____

_____

_____

_____

CHAPTER 17

Using Curiosity to Lean Into Discomfort: Change Doesn't Have to Be Scary

Let's take a look at a story that exemplifies the power of curiosity in overcoming deeply ingrained habits of fear and anxiety. One of my patients, Dave, revealed to me in a session that his father had physically abused him from an early age. This unpredictable violence from his father instilled in Dave a state of perpetual high alert. Constant vigilance became part of Dave's identity. But through mindfulness practices, Dave learned to become curious about his sensations of alertness, asking himself if there was true danger. He found that as he simply observed his feelings with curiosity, they would dissipate.

The key realization for Dave was recognizing that his high alert mode was a learned habit, one that could be unlearned. By being curious about his experiences and verifying whether he was actually in danger, he began to retrain his brain to distinguish between perceived and real threats. This practice, repeated over time, allowed him to shift from a state of anxiety to one of safety and calm.

Dave's journey wasn't without its challenges. Accustomed to anxiety, he found calmness initially discomforting. This discomfort, however, was a sign that he was entering the "growth zone," an area between the known comfort zone and the fear-driven danger zone. Remember, change can be scary—at first. By leaning into this discomfort with curiosity, Dave transformed his experience, ultimately finding comfort in calmness and joy (new habits!).

Interest curiosity (I-curiosity) is central to this process. Unlike deprivation-driven curiosity (D-curiosity), which seeks to fill specific gaps in knowledge and can lead us to a closed-off mental state, I-curiosity is open-ended and expansive, bringing joy to the journey of discovery. It is through this type of curiosity that Dave—and all of us—can continuously learn and grow, shifting from a fixed mindset to a growth mindset.

EXERCISE 1: HIGH ALERT MAPPING

When you feel anxious or on high alert, pause to map out the sensations in your body. Use curiosity to explore these feelings, noting their location, quality, and intensity.

EXERCISE 2: DANGER VS. SAFETY

Create two columns on a page. In one, list instances where you felt anxious without real danger. In the other, note times when there was an actual threat. Reflect on how your body responded in each case.

EXERCISE 3: CURIOSITY

Whenever you feel that closed-down, contracted feeling of anxiety, ask yourself, *Is there real danger here?* Use this practice to observe how often your anxiety is a habit rather than a response to immediate threat.

EXERCISE 4: TAKE A BREATH

Practice the breathing exercise outlined in *Unwinding Anxiety* when you feel anxiety coming on. Here it is again for easy reference. Ask yourself, *How do I know I'm breathing?* and get curious to see where you feel the physical sensations (a silent *hmm* is appropriate here). You might notice the physical sensations of your abdomen moving in and out; you might notice your chest moving if you are a bit nervous and breathing shallowly. Once you've found where you notice your physical sensations of breathing, you can simply continue paying attention to your breathing, or if that gets boring or becomes challenging, amp up the curiosity by watching your body's natural processes that determine your breathing cycle, such as when the inbreath/outbreath stops and reverses course, or how long your body pauses between the in and out breaths.

JOURNAL PROMPT 1: Journal about times you've felt discomfort due to new, nonthreatening situations. Identify how curiosity can turn these moments into opportunities for growth.

_____

_____

_____

_____

_____

JOURNAL PROMPT 2: Reflect on a recent moment of calm. If you're not used to having a lot of moments of calm in your life, how did your body and mind respond to this unfamiliar sensation of safety?

_____

_____

_____

_____

JOURNAL PROMPT 3: Write about a situation in which curiosity helped you move past a habitual response and discuss what you learned from that experience.

_____

_____

_____

_____

JOURNAL PROMPT 4: Think about a "comfortable" but unhelpful habit, like worrying. How can you use curiosity to reassess its value in your life?

_____

_____

_____

JOURNAL PROMPT 5: Describe how incorporating mindfulness into daily activities, like observing your breath, has impacted your ability to remain present and curious.

_____

_____

_____

Curiosity, when embraced, can be a profound tool for transforming habitual responses into opportunities for growth and learning. By mindfully examining our sensations and questioning the reality of perceived dangers, we can rewire our brains to differentiate between false alarms and true threats, allowing us to find comfort in new zones of calm and ease. This process of mindful awareness, especially through curiosity, not only helps us unlearn deeply ingrained habits of anxiety but also encourages a shift from a fixed mindset to a growth mindset, where every moment becomes a potential for learning.

CHAPTER 18

What's Good About Rainy Days?

From my own childhood adventures in deconstructing toys to adulthood revelations about mindfulness and habit change, I've learned the profound impact of applying curiosity to our actions. Diving headfirst into tasks without proper attention led to both minor accidents and significant insights into how we can get caught up in our behaviors. Things like I-curiosity and mindful breathing can be great third-gear practices that disrupt us when we're sucked into an old habit. It can be easy to panic once we recognize that we are falling into a habit loop. But here's the third-gear exercise that helps us stay present and ride those moments out: RAIN.

As a reminder, RAIN stands for:

RECOGNIZE/RELAX into what is arising (for example, a feeling of anxiety).

ACCEPT/ALLOW it to be there.

INVESTIGATE bodily sensations, emotions, and thoughts (get curious).

NOTE what is happening from moment to moment.

This shift from a reactive or panicked response to a curious response transforms our relationship with our environment and ourselves, offering a richer, more engaged experience of the world.

EXERCISE 1: WORKING THE GEARS

Reflect on a habit that typically leads to negative outcomes. Break it down into its trigger, behavior, and result components. How might curiosity alter your response?

EXERCISE 2: RAIN PRACTICE

Next time you encounter a craving or anxiety, apply the RAIN method. Record your experience, noting any shifts in your reaction to or perception of the situation.

EXERCISE 3: CURIOSITY IN ACTION

Choose an activity you do mindlessly. The next time you engage with it, see how much you can see it as fresh and new, focusing deeply on each aspect with curiosity. Document what you discover.

JOURNAL PROMPT 1: Write about a time when not paying attention led to an error. What was your automatic response? How could curiosity have altered the outcome?

_____

_____

_____

_____

_____

JOURNAL PROMPT 2: How has curiosity helped you grow or learn something new recently? Explore the sensations and mindset that accompanied this discovery.

_____

_____

_____

_____

_____

CHAPTER 19

All You Need Is Love

When a thirty-year-old woman struggling with binge-eating disorder came into my outpatient clinic, her history of having been emotionally abused and her subsequent coping mechanism of numbing unpleasant emotions through binge-eating led to a deeply ingrained habit loop. This loop was not only perpetuated by the immediate but fleeting relief of numbing herself from negative emotions but also echoed by feelings of guilt and self-judgment, leading to further binges. Through mapping out these habit loops and introducing curiosity and loving kindness practices, she began to break the cycle, reduce her binge-eating, *and* address her habit of self-judgment. Loving kindness, in particular, offered a sustainable and internally based bigger, better offer by fostering acceptance and warmth toward herself and others, eventually helping her to reclaim her life and find joy.

EXERCISE 1: MAPPING YOUR SELF-JUDGMENT HABIT LOOPS

Identify a self-judgment-related habit you struggle with, breaking it down into triggers, behaviors, and results. Reflect on what you're really getting from this loop.

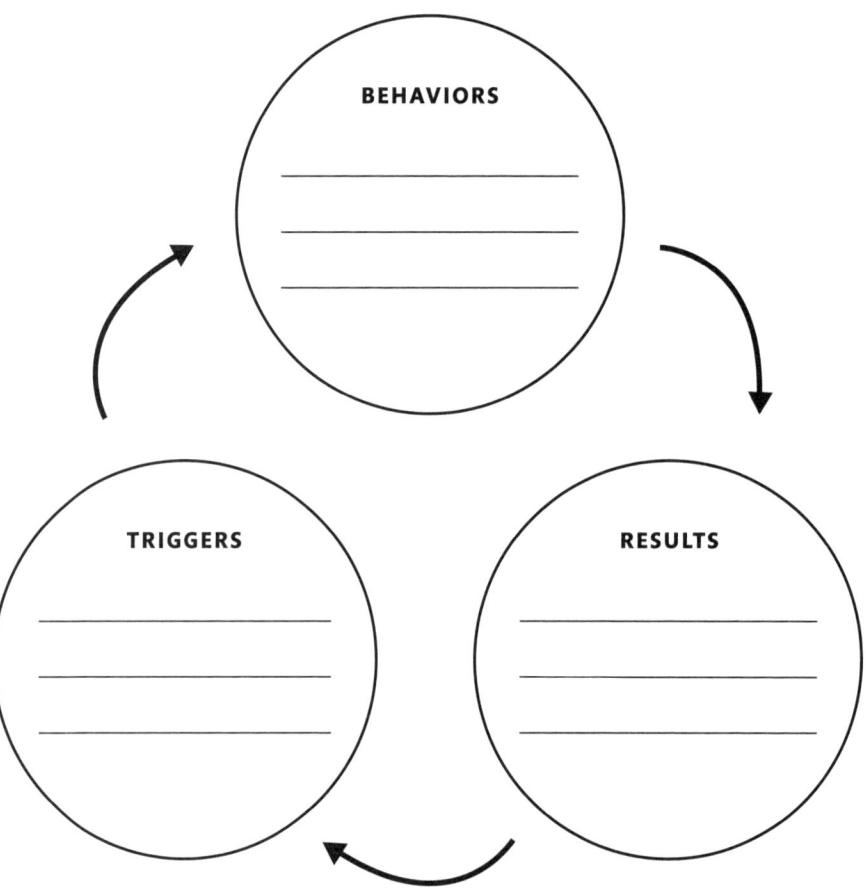

EXERCISE 2: ECHO HABIT LOOP IDENTIFICATION

Think of a habit loop that leads to another, such as feeling guilty after indulging in a habit. Explore how this echo affects your behavior and feelings.

EXERCISE 3: PRACTICING LOVING KINDNESS

Spend a little time each day practicing loving kindness toward yourself and others. Notice any shifts in your mood or overall outlook.

EXERCISE 4: OBSERVING SELF-JUDGMENT

Keep a log of moments when you catch yourself in self-judgment. Practice offering loving kindness in these moments and note any changes in how you feel about yourself.

JOURNAL PROMPT 1: Write about a time when one of your habit loops led to another (for example, worrying triggered a self-judgment habit loop). How did it impact your emotions and behavior?

_____

_____

_____

_____

_____

JOURNAL PROMPT 2: Reflect on your initial resistance or feelings about practicing loving kindness. Has your perception changed over time?

_____

_____

_____

_____

_____

JOURNAL PROMPT 3: How does self-judgment show up in your life? Describe how it influences your habits and your feelings toward yourself.

_____

_____

_____

_____

_____

JOURNAL PROMPT 4: After practicing loving kindness, journal about any changes you've noticed in your relationship with yourself and others. What feels different?

JOURNAL PROMPT 5: Consider the bigger, better offers (BBOs) you've discovered through mindfulness practices. How have they helped you step out of unhelpful habit loops?

Through understanding and mapping out deeply ingrained habit loops, we can begin to unravel the cycles of behavior driven by negative emotions and self-judgment. Introducing mindfulness—specifically the practice of loving kindness—offers a powerful tool for breaking these loops, allowing for self-acceptance and compassion. This transformative approach not only reduces the frequency of undesired behaviors but also fosters a healthier relationship with oneself and others.

CHAPTER 20

The Why Habit Loop

In my clinical practice, I also encountered Amy, who struggled with severe anxiety from trying to manage her responsibilities. Despite attempting to pinpoint the cause of her anxiety, she found herself caught in a why habit loop, exacerbating her distress. When she started feeling anxious, she would often end up questioning why she was anxious in the first place, and her family and friends even gave her the impression they were wondering why she wasn't fixed yet.

I introduced Amy to the practice of mindfulness, focusing on what is happening in the present rather than why it's happening, and encouraged her to employ breathing exercises to break her habit loop. This approach helped her step out of her recursive anxiety patterns by focusing on the present, which underscored the idea that understanding the cause of anxiety is less crucial than managing one's reaction to it. I wrote about Amy because she is emblematic of so many people that I meet who go down the rabbit hole of why instead of focusing on the changeable habit of what.

EXERCISE 1: SKIP THE WHY, MAP THE LOOP

Identify a recent situation where you felt overwhelmed or anxious. Map out the trigger, behavior, and result, focusing on the present experience rather than searching for a root cause.

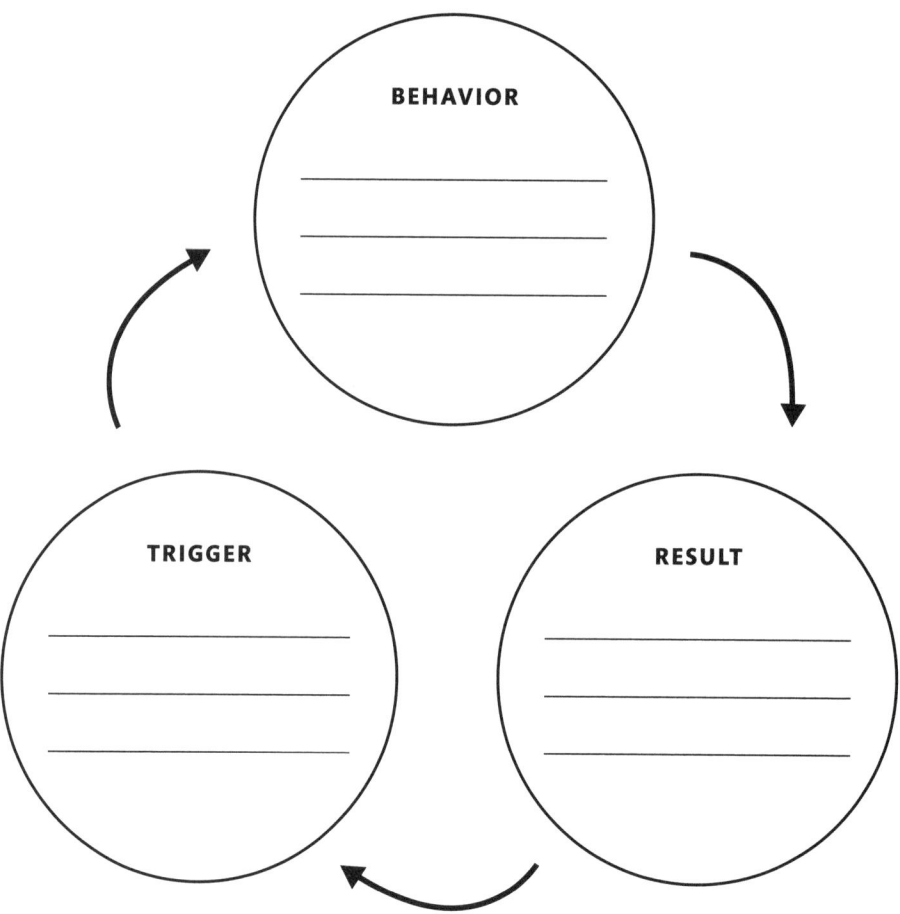

EXERCISE 2: BREATHING EXERCISE TO BREAK THE WHY LOOP

Practice taking three deep breaths whenever you find yourself spiraling into the why of your emotions. With each exhale, mentally remind yourself that why doesn't matter, focusing instead on what you're feeling at the moment.

EXERCISE 3: EYE-WIDENING PRACTICE

Next time you feel a surge of negative emotion, consciously open your eyes really wide for ten seconds. Note any changes in the intensity or nature of your emotion, reinforcing the shift from frustration or anxiety to curiosity.

JOURNAL PROMPT 1: Describe a recent event that led you into a why habit loop. How did this focus on finding a cause affect your anxiety or stress levels?

_____

_____

_____

_____

_____

JOURNAL PROMPT 2: After trying the breathing exercise or the eye-widening practice, reflect on how these methods influenced your emotional state. Did they help you step out of the habit loop? How did your perspective on the situation change?

_____

_____

_____

_____

_____

JOURNAL PROMPT 3: Write about a moment when curiosity led you to a positive outcome or a deeper understanding of yourself or a situation. How did opening yourself to curiosity change the way you dealt with the emotion or challenge?

_____

_____

_____

_____

_____

JOURNAL PROMPT 4: After practicing opening your eyes wide in moments of distress, reflect on any shifts in your emotional experience. Were you able to engage more effectively with the present? How did this physical action impact your mental state?

_____

_____

_____

_____

_____

JOURNAL PROMPT 5: Reflect on how adopting a focus on what rather than why has influenced your approach to anxiety or other challenging emotions. What have you learned about yourself and your habit loops through this process?

_____

_____

_____

_____

CHAPTER 21

Noting Practice

Using mindfulness to shift from reactionary patterns to a more responsive, aware state is akin to navigating through life with a map instead of wandering aimlessly. The practice of loving kindness, for example, allows us to step outside self-judgmental loops, while RAIN (Recognize, Allow, Investigate, Note) offers a structured approach to managing the urge for something like late-night snacking.

The challenge, however, lies in our habitual reactions to discomfort—our automatic shift to autopilot, driven by an aversion to unpleasant feelings.

Let's consider the power of bringing an accepting, curious awareness to our experiences. When we are caught in habitual reactivity, such as the compulsion to do something as a means to feel better, we miss the essence of simply being. Curiosity about our reactions to fear and anxiety can be transformative, propelling us from a state of constant doing to one of being. This shift is crucial for hacking our reward-based learning system, allowing us to replace habitual reactions with mindful responses.

Our feeling body is much stronger (and wiser) than our thinking brain. Pragmatically, we have to feel—in our bodies—how rewarding (or unrewarding) a behavior is. This builds disenchantment with unhelpful habits, and it strengthens helpful ones (e.g., third-gear practices) because they are rewarding in themselves. I've never had a patient come to my clinic with the chief complaint of too much curiosity or that they are addicted to kindness. Just sayin' . . .

EXERCISE 1: NOTING PRACTICE

Practice noting for thirty seconds three times a day. Start with times that you're naturally waiting for something (for example, while food or drink is heating in the microwave, while you are sitting at a stoplight in a car, while you are walking from one place to another).

EXERCISE 2: LOVING KINDNESS MEDITATION

Practice sending loving kindness to yourself and then to someone you have neutral feelings toward. Note the differences in how you feel before and after the practice.

EXERCISE 3: THE CURIOSITY SHIFT

Spend a day noting every time you react automatically to a situation. Later, reflect on how you could have responded with curiosity instead.

EXERCISE 4: EXPLORING AUTOPILOT

Choose a routine activity (e.g., brushing your teeth) and focus on doing it with full awareness for one week. Note any changes in your experience of the activity.

Now let's reflect on how our third-gear practices can be implemented more and how they've served us well.

JOURNAL PROMPT 1 Reflect on a recent time you reacted out of habit to an unpleasant emotion. What was the trigger, and what could a curious response have looked like?

_____

_____

_____

_____

_____

JOURNAL PROMPT 2: Describe a situation where practicing loving kindness could change your habitual reaction to a person or event.

_____

_____

_____

_____

_____

JOURNAL PROMPT 3: Recall an instance where you felt like a "human doing" rather than a "human being." Was there something you were avoiding feeling or dealing with? How might being with yourself—relating differently to your thoughts, emotions, and body sensations—change the outcome in future situations that are similar?

_____

_____

_____

_____

_____

JOURNAL PROMPT 4: Imagine your life as it would be if curiosity replaced your most challenging habit loop. What would this situation look like, and how would it feel different?

_____

_____

_____

_____

_____

JOURNAL PROMPT 5: Reflect on the "trying too hard" paradox in shifting habits. Can you identify a time when letting go of effort led to more ease in change?

_____

_____

_____

_____

By engaging in these exercises and prompts, we start to disentangle the intricate web of habits that keep us in reactive modes, paving the way for a more mindful, intentional way of being that is rooted in curiosity and kindness.

Evidence-Based Faith

The best evidence you can gather is your own experience: what you've seen, felt, and experienced while doing the practices that you've been learning from *Unwinding Anxiety*. That's the only way that you develop an unshakable faith that you can do it. Remember, this doesn't mean that you won't ever have anxiety again (I still do!), but you will know how to work with it, even if that moment feels a little turbulent or shaky.

As we near the end of our journey—that is of learning the concepts, as your journey into building a lifetime of curiosity and kindness has just begun—I want to pose a question: Have you found your unique mantra or reminder—like "I think I can," the refrain of the Little Engine That Could—to bring mindfulness into your daily life? This phrase or thought can serve as your mindfulness bell, a cue signaling a shift into a more aware and responsive state. The transformation from old habits to new, more rewarding behaviors is rooted in practice, much like preparing for a test. The key here is a dedication to practicing the newer behaviors until they become second nature. Through consistent practice, we learn to navigate the anxious feelings accompanying urges and worries and to embrace the expansiveness that kindness and curiosity offer.

EXERCISE 1: FINDING YOUR MINDFULNESS MANTRA

Reflect on phrases or thoughts that resonate deeply with you and write them down. Practice saying your chosen mantra in moments of stress or distraction to bring yourself back to awareness in the present moment.

EXERCISE 2: THE TRIGGER TRANSFORMATION

Identify a daily occurrence that often leads to automatic, habitual responses. Use this as your mindfulness bell, a cue to shift into a more mindful gear, and observe the results.

EXERCISE 3: MAPPING EXPANSION VS. CONTRACTION

Throughout your day, note moments of contraction (stress, anxiety) and expansion (joy, curiosity). Observe how different triggers and responses lead to these sensations.

Another way to look at this is that this is just the beginning. Wisdom comes from experience, and concepts simply lay the path for that experience. So you've got the concepts, and now it's time to walk that path, experiencing things on your own and fostering the development of wisdom as you go.

EXERCISE 4: KEEP A JOURNAL FOR A WEEK

Journal throughout the course of your week, noting each instance where mindfulness practices help you navigate challenges. Use this as a way to build your evidence-based faith in the process.

JOURNAL PROMPT 1: Reflect on the concept of evidence-based faith. What evidence have you gathered so far that demonstrates the effectiveness of mindfulness in your life?

_____

_____

_____

_____

_____

JOURNAL PROMPT 2: Reflect on a recent situation where you successfully shifted from a habitual reaction to a mindful response. What mantra or thought helped you make this shift?

_____

_____

_____

_____

_____

JOURNAL PROMPT 3: Consider a recurring trigger in your daily life. How can you transform this into a mindfulness cue to shift gears?

_____

_____

_____

_____

JOURNAL PROMPT 4: How has the practice of observing your reactions and cultivating curiosity impacted your day-to-day life? Provide specific examples.

_____

_____

_____

_____

_____

By engaging with these exercises and prompts, we continue to forge a path of mindfulness, curiosity, and kindness. Each step, each practice, moves us away from reactive habits and toward a life lived with intention and awareness. Keep practicing, keep noting, and let your accumulated evidence guide you toward a future where mindfulness is not just a practice, but a way of being.

CHAPTER 23

Anxiety Sobriety

In a weekly live online video group, Dr. Robin Boudette and I engage with individuals from across the globe, diving into their struggles and exploring pathways to overcoming their challenges. This real-time interaction offers a unique and practical approach to mindfulness, rooted in the principles of curiosity, kindness, and the power of now. Our discussions often reveal a common thread: the daunting task of sustaining calm and mindfulness throughout the day, beyond fleeting moments of relief. This reflects a broader challenge faced by many who find the prospect of continuous change overwhelming.

The principle of "one day at a time," borrowed from Alcoholics Anonymous, offers a powerful approach to tackling this challenge. It emphasizes the importance of focusing on the present moment, breaking down the journey into manageable steps. This perspective not only aids in overcoming addiction but also incorporates a valuable framework for addressing anxiety and habitual patterns. It underscores the importance of curiosity and kindness in each moment, encouraging a shift from worrying about the future to engaging fully with the present. We may never be able to stop anxiety from coming on, but we do have control over our response—worrying (and other habitual behaviors) are optional. We can "sober up" from these habits.

EXERCISE 1: MINDFULNESS MANTRA DEVELOPMENT

Continue to reflect on phrases that ground you in the present moment, and practice using them throughout your day, especially in moments of stress or anxiety.

EXERCISE 2: BREAKING DOWN THE DAY

Choose a day to consciously break down into hours or even moments. Note how this approach affects your anxiety levels and your ability to remain present.

EXERCISE 3: THE "ONE DAY AT A TIME" CHALLENGE

For one week, start each day with the commitment to stay mindful and present, using the "one day at a time" mantra to guide you.

JOURNAL PROMPT 1: Reflect on a time when focusing on the present moment helped you navigate a challenging situation. How did it change your experience?

_____

_____

_____

_____

JOURNAL PROMPT 2: How does the mantra "one moment at a time" and/or "short moments, many times" resonate with your journey toward mindfulness? Can you identify moments when applying this principle would have been beneficial?

_____

_____

_____

_____

JOURNAL PROMPT 3: Consider the concept of "anxiety sobriety." What does it mean to you, and how can you apply it in your daily life?

_____

_____

_____

_____

_____

JOURNAL PROMPT 4: Reflect on the role of curiosity and kindness in your journey toward overcoming habitual patterns. How have these qualities impacted your progress?

_____

_____

_____

_____

JOURNAL PROMPT 5: Envision a future where you apply the "one day at a time" approach consistently. What changes do you anticipate in your life?

_____

_____

_____

In this journey of mindfulness, we are reminded of the power of the present moment and the transformative potential of adopting a "one moment at a time" mentality. This approach, grounded in the practices of curiosity, kindness, and present-moment awareness (practiced short moments, many times), not only offers a pathway out of anxiety and habitual patterns but also paves the way for a more connected and fulfilling life. Onward!

Appendix: Behavioral Tendencies Quiz

Please rank the following in the order that is most consistent with how you *generally* behave (not how you think you *should* behave or how you *might* behave in a very specific situation). You should give your first and initial response without thinking about the question too much. Place a 1 by the answer that best fits you, followed by a 2 for your second choice, and a 3 for the answer that least fits you.

1. If I were to plan a party, . . .

   ☐ I would want it to be high-energy, with lots of people.
   ☐ I would want only certain people there.
   ☐ it would be last-minute and free-form.

2. When it comes to cleaning my room, I . . .

☐ take pride in making things look great.

☐ quickly notice problems, imperfections, or untidiness.

☐ don't tend to notice or get bothered by clutter.

3. I prefer to make my living space . . .

☐ beautiful.

☐ organized.

☐ creatively chaotic.

4. When doing my job, I like to . . .

☐ be passionate and energetic.

☐ make sure everything is accurate.

☐ consider future possibilities/wonder about the best way forward.

5. When talking to people, I might come across as . . .

☐ affectionate.

☐ realistic.

☐ philosophical.

6. The disadvantage of my clothing style is that it may be . . .

☐ decadent.

☐ unimaginative.

☐ mismatched or uncoordinated.

7. In general, I carry myself . . .

☐ buoyantly.

☐ briskly.

☐ aimlessly.

8. My room is . . .

☐ richly decorated.

☐ neatly arranged.

☐ messy.

9. Generally, I tend to . . .

☐ have a strong desire for things.

☐ be critical but clear-thinking.

☐ be in my own world.

10. At school, I was known for . . .

☐ having lots of friends.

☐ being intellectual.

☐ daydreaming.

11. I usually wear clothes in a way that is . . .

☐ fashionable and attractive.

☐ neat and orderly.

☐ carefree.

12. I come across as . . .

☐ affectionate.

☐ thoughtful.

☐ absent-minded.

13. When other people are enthusiastic about something, I . . .

☐ jump on board and want to get involved.

☐ tend to be skeptical of it.

☐ go off on tangents.

Now add up the numbers to get a crude score for each of the top options, middle options, and bottom options. The option with the lowest score equals the greatest tendency.

Top = approach type; Middle = avoid type; Bottom = go-with-the-flow type. For example, if you scored an 18 for the top option, a 25 for the middle option, and a 35 for the bottom option, you have a much higher tendency for the approach type.

Acknowledgments

I'd like to thank all my patients and people in the Unwinding Anxiety program with whom I've had the honor of working over the past decade. I have learned a tremendous amount from them and continue to grow from each interaction. I'd also like to thank Jacqui Barnett and Rob Suhoza for their careful read of this manuscript and thoughtful feedback.